FREEBODY

""FreeBody *introduces us to a complex system in a simple way. Cat Matlock's voice is gentle and humorous and clearly genuine. This book is like an offering, inviting the reader to learn a method for truly healing themselves. She has taught me that freedom from pain is attainable. This book is a must read."*

—MICHELLE ASSOIAN

"Cat's FreeBody technique is a must for anyone that is caring for their body and for others. This book teaches simple and effective ways to release any tension held in the body."

—EILEEN GERTZ, LMBT

"FreeBody is a must-read if you've ever experienced acute or chronic pain. Cat does an excellent job explaining how trigger points, fascia, and stress are the roots of pain, and how you can help yourself to get FREE! This work is truly life-changing."

—AMY HOWARD, FNP-C

"In her new book, Cat Matlock brings together the latest research, along with her thirty years of experience, to help in understanding the intricacies of the human body. Hope and healing resonate throughout the pages. Highly recommended!"

—JANIS WILLIAMS, CERTIFIED ESSENTRICS INSTRUCTOR

FREEBODY

THE BODY, PAIN, AND A
PATH TO FREEDOM

CAT MATLOCK

MANUSCRIPTS
PRESS

FREEBODY

The Body, Pain, and a Path to Freedom

ISBN   979-8-88926-740-9   *Paperback*

979-8-88926-741-6   *Ebook*

Contents

Introduction

You wake up feeling achy. You get up and wonder if your body is going to give you trouble again. Or maybe you didn't sleep well because that pain kept waking you up.

You wonder, will my sciatica be bad today? Will my neck freeze up? Is today the day that old back injury returns? Or maybe you just know things will hurt. And you can't fully live the life you are meant to live because your body keeps getting in the way. Does this sound familiar?

I am often struck by how many of those who come to me for help are suffering needlessly. They have pain or dysfunction in their bodies that they just can't figure out. Their physical therapist, chiropractor, doctor, massage therapist, or yoga teacher can't seem to figure it out either.

It is tiresome to try all kinds of treatments without real improvement, not to mention the costs in cash and time. In the end, many people are told to either just deal with it, take anti-inflammatories or pain killers, have surgery, or accept that they are "getting old" and this is just how they are going to feel. By the time people come to me, they're exhausted and worried.

I see the same patterns over and over again. I've worked on folks with the same types of back aches, the same sciatica symptoms, the same neck pain and headaches time and again. Each situation is unique, yet the symptoms are common, and with the right tools, pain goes away.

We need a new paradigm in addressing musculoskeletal pain. Neck and back pain take first prize in annual healthcare spending according to a 2020 report in the *Journal of the American Medical Association*. More money was spent on neck and back pain *than any other health concern*. Their recent reports showed a yearly cost of almost $135 billion paid for neck and back pain alone. Spending on "other musculoskeletal disorders" came in second place at just under $130 billion, and diabetes spending was third (2020, 863-884). That's almost $265 billion dollars spent on muscle and bone pain in one year in the US alone.

Many people suffering with pain end up at a doctor's office seeking understanding, a diagnosis, and relief. Far too often, those people have been prescribed opioids to get rid of their pain.

We have learned the hard way that opioid medicines are not the answer, with 75 percent of all drug overdose deaths in 2020 involving opioids and 1.6 million people diagnosed with an "opioid use disorder" that same year (US Dept. of Health and Human Services 2020). Fortunately, increased awareness, and even lawsuits, have slowed the over-prescribing of opioids. But they were never the answer to begin with. Masking the pain is never the way to true freedom. Yes, for some, pain drugs can give you enough relief to stop the pain cycle and get you moving again. For those people, pain meds can help on the road to freedom. But it's risky and, again, they are never the final answer.

Most of the folks I see who are over forty are worried they are in that "getting old so just live with it" phase of life. They ache. Old injuries come back to visit and often stick around. Some of the people I work with feel like victims of their own bodies. They say things like, "My body has failed me." Or, "My body is pissing me off! I'm so mad. I'm so sick of this nagging shoulder!" Or they say, "I can't sleep. I can't get comfortable. And that's just causing me more stress and I can't take it anymore." And I get it. They feel imprisoned by their neck, back, or hips and haven't found the relief they crave. I can relate because I felt that way when I had chronic sciatica. But that's gone now. At fifty-three, I feel better in my body than I did in my twenties.

What I have learned is that the human body is a miraculous healing wonder. It wants to heal and is always striving toward that. If we understand a bit about how the body works, and how to create the conditions for healing, most people get much better. Many can be completely pain free. Old injuries don't have to come back full force because you can nip them in the bud. If you do get injured, you can take steps to clear the pain from your body, and your brain, and fully recover.

I have spent my life learning about pain, the body, and healing through trigger-point work, yoga, meditation, trauma-informed yoga therapy, and other trauma-informed healing modalities. Over the past thirty years, I have worked with thousands of people helping them to get out of pain. We are fortunate to be in a time of greater understanding of the brain and the effect that our emotional and mental landscape has on our bodies and the pain we feel. I am grateful for the many people who have trusted me with their stories and suffering.

This book will introduce you to three key systems that go awry and cause pain: muscles and trigger points, fascia, and the brain on stress. Once you understand how these three systems produce the pain we feel, you'll learn the five elements of the FreeBody System to address that pain. I developed Free-Body from what I saw working time and again when others asked me for help. I have found that when you put these tools and knowledge into action, you can feel much better, or even be pain free, in a relatively short amount of time.

You'll meet one client who came to me after seventy years of headaches who doesn't suffer headaches anymore. You'll meet a young woman with chronic lower back pain who was able to get rid of it quickly and completely. You'll hear the steps my clients took to relieve their neck issues, hip pain, and more. You'll learn how I was finally able to get rid of chronic sciatica that had plagued me for over fifteen years. And when you do fall or have an injury in the future, you'll understand how to follow the best path for healing.

Take Lorelai. Lorelai is an acupuncturist who had been unable to sit down without terrible pain for over ten months.

In her forties, she had started working out again. She was feeling great until one day when she swung a kettlebell a little too hard, which led to a bulging disc in her lower back. After that injury, she experienced terrible pain in her buttocks, which radiated down the back of her thigh when she sat down. Lorelai stood all day long, which also was uncomfortable, to avoid the terrible pain she felt when she sat down.

Lorelai tried a lot of therapies but didn't improve. After I evaluated her and told her that yes indeed there was hope she'd be fine again, she cried. "That makes so much sense! No one has ever explained it like that before." Within the week, she was able to sit pain free, and after a couple of months, she was completely healed. This is exactly how I want your story to end.

This book is for you and your body. It's for anyone who slips or falls and wants to be able to get back up again. It's for anyone who wants to age well without worrying about "that old back injury" and for anyone who is suffering with that injury flare-up. If you're experiencing chronic pain right now, you'll learn essential steps to significantly increase your chances to be pain free.

After just one session, I often hear, "I finally feel hopeful that I'm not going to live the rest of my life with this pain." I explain all the parts of the FreeBody System, the Five Points of Freedom, and it makes sense to them. Just that understanding is helpful! There is not one quick fix for persistent aches and pains. You need a system to support your healing journey, and that's what I offer you here.

Many get better quickly and are surprised after suffering for years and trying a multitude of healthcare professionals. They lost hope, and that made everything worse. I want you to have hope. *Nothing* is hopeless. You *can* feel better. I am here to help you understand how.

Welcome to FreeBody.

PART 1

TRIGGER POINTS

CHAPTER 1

Muscles and Trigger Points

We begin our journey to understand pain by exploring muscles and trigger points. You'll learn what causes muscles to feel tense and tight and why they become weak and less mobile. You'll learn what causes muscles to ache, and why sometimes the pain you feel isn't actually coming from the place where you feel it.

With some basic knowledge of trigger points, pieces of the pain puzzle begin to fall into place. This knowledge is a kind of liberation. It will help demystify your pain and support you in taking steps to becoming pain free. I believe that a large part of what we call aging is actually chronically held trigger points in our muscles. Read this if you want to age well!

CHAPTER 2

What Is a Trigger Point?

When your trigger points release, the relief can feel like magic! Trigger points are those tender spots that you always want your massage therapist, or whoever rubs your shoulders, to find. When they press into one, you might say, "That's it! That's the spot!" A trigger point is a focal point of tension in a muscle that causes pain, inflammation, and limits your mobility. It is a part of your muscle that is stuck in contraction and doesn't relax when it should (Travell, Simons, and Simons 1999). Trigger points can make your muscles feel "tense" and "tight." Trigger points hurt when you press on them but can cause pain and aching even when you're not touching them at all.

For thirty years I have focused on trigger points as a source of pain and pain relief. I have found working with trigger points to be a very effective approach to reduce pain in my own body and those of my clients. When you understand trigger points and their pain referral patterns, meaning where they cause you pain, you have a wonderful guide to support your healing. I'll offer you some tips on how to find and release your trigger points at the end of the book and provide you with a website (www.FreeBodyBook.com) and a YouTube channel (@CatMatlock) where you can get further help. But first you need to understand some things about trigger points themselves.

Releasing trigger points is often the essential piece missing in the care of the people I help. Trigger points are a common reason people experience pain or loss of mobility, and the symptoms increase over time and spread to other areas. However, if someone is doing great trigger-point-release work, and the trigger points keep coming back, it means that the conditions that created the trigger points haven't been addressed. That's why I created the FreeBody System: so others can understand the root causes of trigger points like stress, posture, and lack of movement. A common reason trigger points return is that there are more muscles contributing to the problem than those being treated. Our bodies move as a symphony of things working together, never just one muscle on its own. Trigger points do not exist in a vacuum; they activate tension in other muscles, and they are persistent. They can get stuck in your muscles and stay stuck there for years, even decades, if not addressed (Travell, Simons, and Simons 1999).

SEVENTY YEARS OF HEADACHES GONE!

Several years ago, I worked with a client in her seventies suffering from chronic headaches. When Carmen came up to my office, she moved slowly and had an air of defeat about her. Being in pain all the time wears a person down.

When she sat to tell me her story, she said, "I don't really believe you can help me, but my friend was so insistent that I see you because you helped her so much with her back, I figured I would give it a try. So here I am." She shared that she couldn't remember a time in her life when she had gone longer than twenty-four hours without a headache. She recalled being a little girl, just about two or three, curled up in her grandma's lap and crying because her head hurt so much. That headache persisted to the very day I met her nearly seventy years later. She had tried everything to get rid of her headaches, even traveled to other countries in search of treatments and cures, but nothing ever really helped for long.

I've heard similar stories too many times to count. Many people come to me exasperated and in pain. They have run the gamut of therapies looking for answers. Most have been to physical therapists, doctors, specialists, and some to acupuncturists and a variety of massage therapists. Their healthcare team grows over time. They might get some relief, but the ache doesn't fully go away and, at some point, it returns with a vengeance. They often get diagnosed with something like migraines, bursitis, some kind of joint problem, or get prescribed pain meds to deal with it. They are all tired of it. They just want to feel better. Carmen had basically given up, but a little part of her was hopeful she would find the key to feeling better. I really wanted to help her.

I spent two hours with Carmen, working through my protocol, adjusting it to her body and needs. When she left, she did not have a headache. But she'd received momentary relief before and the headache always returned, so she was skeptical. We would see. I taught her about the trigger points in her neck and shoulders that I believed to be causing her symptoms. I shared reasons her trigger points might come back and ways to avoid that happening. I also showed her how to release her own trigger points in her chest, neck, and the top of her shoulders so she could keep releasing the spots causing her pain.

Then I didn't hear from her. I felt badly because I really wanted to help and figured that our session didn't keep her headache away. Dang. Sometimes a person comes in and I hear their story, their suffering, and I want to help them so badly I almost ache. I felt that way for Carmen. I was sad to have not helped her. That is until a few weeks later when I received a call.

"Cat! Oh, Cat with the magic hands!" she sang out on the phone. She explained that her headache did try to return a couple of days after our session but she "squeezed those nasty little points" as I taught her, and the headache went away. She'd gone two full weeks headache free. Two full weeks! She'd never been longer than twenty-four hours in her life without a headache! She wanted to come see me for a follow up before going on a trip with her husband. They were to travel for the first time in their whole adult lives *not* to look for a doctor or a remedy but just to enjoy a vacation.

The effect of receiving good trigger-point work can seem like a miracle. But trigger points can, and often do, coexist with other issues that cause pain. While they are often a really big piece of the story, they are rarely the entire story. This is why some people experience excellent trigger-point-release work and still end up with persistent pain. As I said earlier, to really release trigger points and keep them away, you must also change the conditions that created them. The FreeBody System addresses the main causes of trigger points.

SO WHAT IS A TRIGGER POINT?

Trigger Points became famous through the work of Dr. Janet Travell. While Dr. Travell was in medical school, her shoulder hurt. No doctor could figure out what was wrong with her shoulder.

I read an interview with Dr. Travell, and she shared that in an attempt to get rid of this shoulder pain, she reached around to her shoulder blade, found a very tender spot that, when she pressed on it, reproduced her symptoms all the way down her arm. She said, "It didn't match any known pain pattern of nerve root or segmental distribution or that of any peripheral nerve; it was an independent pattern" (Journal of Clinical Orthodontics 1989). Thus began her long journey of discovering and mapping trigger points in the body. Dr. Travell became famous when her trigger-point work allowed John F. Kennedy to heal chronic back pain and eventually become president. As president, he appointed Dr. Travell the first female White House doctor in history.

The classic textbook definition of a trigger point comes from *Myofascial Pain and Dysfunction: The Trigger Point Manual* by Drs. Janet Travell and David Simons. Travell and Simons define a trigger point as "a highly irritable localized spot of exquisite tenderness in a nodule in a palpable taut band of muscle tissue" (Travell, Simons, and Simons 1999, 5).

"Exquisite tenderness" means that the point hurts when you touch it. A "palpable taut band of muscle tissue" means that you can feel a place in the tissue where that section of the muscle is pulled long and taut. It's thicker than the tissue around it. It gets pulled taut because the trigger point is in the center of that band of muscle fibers, contracting in toward the center, and the taut bands are the outer portions of the muscle fibers that are being constantly pulled by the part that's contracting. The center, the trigger point, is drawing everything in toward itself and the outer edges of the fibers are anchored, so the outer parts get stretched and pulled long and taut.

Have you ever found a painful knot in your own body? And even though it hurt to press on it, you perhaps also felt relief? Yeah. That's a trigger point.

We don't fully understand everything about trigger points. What we do know is that trigger points do occur and they can be what's behind your loss of range of motion, weakness in an area of your body, or that nagging ache that wakes you up in the middle of the night. "Pain clinic doctors skilled at detecting and treating trigger points have found that they're the primary cause of pain roughly 75 percent of the time, and they play at least a part in virtually every pain problem" (C. Davies and A. Davies 2004, 2).

I spoke with Amber Davies, who co-authored *The Trigger Point Therapy Workbook,* a trigger-point self-treatment manual, with her father, Clair Davies. She said that a trigger point is a tender spot that "the harder you press on it, the more it hurts. When you lighten up, the sensation is less." That's a key indicator that you've found a trigger point.

So a trigger point is a part of the muscle that is stuck in contraction, it's got a taut band on either side of it, and it hurts when you press on it. It's typically small, at least at first. It can grow to be a bigger and thicker area as more of the muscle gets stuck in contraction. Ouch!

When a trigger point forms, a host of reactions takes place. I'm going to give you a basic understanding so you get excited about releasing your trigger points because we've all got them and they may be wreaking havoc on your body right now, even if you are not in pain.

WHAT'S GOING ON IN THERE?

ENERGY DEPLETION

When that spot gets stuck in contraction, it becomes a drain on the energy available for the muscle to do its job. Muscles contract to create movement and stability. The energy a muscle uses to contract is called ATP, or adenosine triphosphate. ATP comes from fats and sugars that are stored in your body. In a nutshell, when your muscle wants to contract, it grabs ATP from fats and sugars, and the muscle then has the energy to contract (Hultman and Greenhaff 1991).

Every time a muscle—or actually, a *part* of a muscle—contracts, it uses ATP to do that. If a part of your muscle is stuck in contraction, it's constantly using energy. This depletes the energy available to that muscle. This is one reason a muscle with trigger points can become weak.

When I suffered with sciatica symptoms, my right hip was often weak. Sometimes I couldn't stand fully on my right leg to pull up my pants on the left side. I'd go to stand on the right leg and my hip would "give out" and I'd have to sit down to pull my pants up. My glutes on the right side were loaded with trigger points which were causing me sciatica-like pain and which weakened my glutes. Once I got rid of those trigger points, I was immediately stronger. Immediately. And I could stand with full weight on my right leg.

When I was teaching a yoga and foam rolling class years ago, a woman came in and was having hip weakness. As the class was about to do poses which required the participants to stand on one leg at a time, this woman told me she could do the poses on the right side, but not on the left. "But I'm getting help for it," she said. "I'm working with a yoga therapist."

I asked for how long.

"Eight months."

"Eight months and it's still not better?" I asked. I gave her a ball and some instructions and told her to try trigger point release on some key spots. Within minutes, she could fully stand on her left leg.

Do you experience something similar? Maybe one side of your body feels stronger than the other? One hip "gives out" or one knee buckles? An ankle feels weak and it happens to be the ankle you sprained ten years ago so you figure the damage is still there and you'll never recover?

Most of the time, you can recover. I call trigger points "black hole energy suckers" because they are. But if you release those trigger points, your muscles will be stronger because those trigger points will no longer be sucking out energy. Often you'll feel stronger immediately.

INFLAMMATORY CELLS AND OTHER ICKY THINGS

Multiple studies have evaluated cells from around trigger points as well as around healthy tissues to compare the chemical environments of the two. One of those studies found the cellular environment around trigger points was quite measurably different than around non-trigger-point areas. The researchers found that the environment around trigger points was measurably acidic, around a pH of 3 which is the acidity of orange juice (Shah et al. 2008).

An acidic environment has been demonstrated to create fatigue in muscle tissue. In another interesting study, researchers found that lowering the pH level from 7.4 (normal) to 6.4 decreased a muscle fiber's ability to contract significantly, with certain functions reducing as much as 80 percent! In every aspect of the muscle's ability to contract in a lowered pH of 6.4, the muscle fibers were far weaker and less able to utilize ATP, causing fatigue. I'd like to remind you that the pH level found near trigger points in the above study was a pH of 3. Less than half of that 6.4 (Debold et al.

2008). The acidic environment is another reason for weakness in a muscle with trigger points.

Acidosis, or an acidic environment in the tissue, also contributes significantly to pain. Pain is a protector in the body (much more on that later), and it makes sense that the body would generate pain when there is an acidic environment because cells cannot function well in that low pH. Acidosis has been proven as a cause of persistent pain (Lin et al. 2018). Since trigger points appear to generate an acidic state in the tissue, the body is going to react with pain. Trigger points cause pain. Sometimes that pain goes to unlikely places, as we shall soon see.

When the scientists looked at the cells from around the trigger points, they not only found a significantly acidic environment, but they also found a host of pro-inflammatory cells. They reported, "There is a unique biochemical milieu of substances associated with pain and inflammation in the vicinity of an active MTP (myofascial trigger point)" (Shah et al. 2008).

This could be another explanation for why pressing on the trigger point actually hurts. It's inflamed, it's acidic, and the tissue is definitely not happy with what's going on. So it hurts.

CHAPTER 3

Types of Trigger Points

Trigger points are sneaky. Often they cause pain. Typically they limit your range of motion, with or without pain. Sometimes they can make you think you've got a nerve compressed somewhere. Sometimes they can actually lead to a true nerve compression when they tighten the muscle down on a nerve or slide a disc off center, which then compresses the nerve. Sometimes they make your hip or knee "give out." They can cause you to have a headache or that deep ache in your butt or shoulder that wakes you up when you lie on your side. They can make your hands go numb. Often the ache you feel isn't even where the trigger point is. See what I mean? Sneaky.

LATENT AND ACTIVE TRIGGER POINTS

It's important to understand that trigger points do not always cause you to feel pain. You could, and probably do, have trigger points that limit your range of motion. Stew Wild, a trigger point therapy instructor of mine, confirmed this. You will meet him later on. Some trigger points only cause pain when you press on them and others cause pain regardless, but both have an effect on your mobility. Trigger points in one muscle also affect the ability of other muscles to do their jobs. Let's explore.

A **latent trigger point** is a spot in the muscle that is stuck in contraction and can create stiffness and loss of range of motion (Mense and Simons 2001, 206). It will affect other muscles and the joints it acts on (muscle move joints) and it does not cause you to feel an ache or pain. A latent trigger point only hurts when you press on it. In the study I referred to in the last chapter where they extracted fluids from around trigger points, they took samples from both latent and active trigger point areas. The acidosis and pro-inflammatory cells were found around the active trigger points but not around the latent ones. Latent trigger points can make you feel like you have "tension" in a muscle. The muscle just feels tight. I often hear my clients say, "I hold all my tension in my neck and shoulders." Do you feel that? Do you feel "tense" in your neck and shoulders? That means you most likely have latent trigger points there. If that tension then turns into neck pain or a headache, or some other pain referral pattern, that means the trigger points have now become active.

Active trigger points are the ones causing you to ache and feel pain. "Patients with active myofascial (myo is muscle and fascial is fascia) trigger points usually complain of poorly localized, regional, aching pain in the subcutaneous (beneath the skin) tissues, including muscles and joints (Travell,

Simons, and Simons 1999, 20). Active trigger points don't need to be pressed on for you to feel the pain or sensation that is associated with them. You just feel it. Sometimes you might feel it more than others, but there may always be an ache, or sensation, that doesn't fully go away. An active trigger point in your upper trapezius muscle, the most superficial muscle in the upper back, shoulder, and neck area, causes an aching along the side of your neck and headaches on the side of your head. Ever feel neck tension on the side of your neck and find yourself rubbing it incessantly, and stretching your neck, but that doesn't help? Right. Because the ache you feel is coming from the upper trapezius at the top of your shoulder. If you don't release that trigger point, your neck won't feel better.

Here's a picture of the pain pattern of trigger points in the upper trapezius. The lines point to where the trigger points are located, given that everyone's anatomy is slightly different. The shading shows where people with those trigger points indicated they feel the pain referral. Deeper shading means more people have reported pain in that spot. The darker shading does not indicate intensity of pain, but frequency of pain site reported. Your symptoms could be anywhere there is shading.

Active trigger points cause discomfort that you feel all the time, even when you are just sitting or sleeping. When you press on them, they *really* hurt.

Latent trigger points can become active if the muscle is "abused" as described by Mense and Simons in their 2001 book *Muscle Pain: Understanding its Nature, Diagnosis, and*

TRAPEZIUS PAIN REFERRAL PATTERN

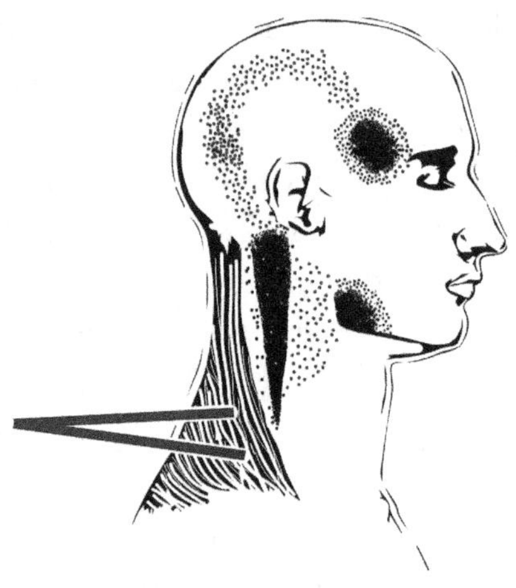

Common pain referral pattern of the upper trapezius. The lines point to where the trigger points tend to develop. The shading indicates where people who have those trigger points report that they feel pain or sensation; neck and jaw pain, pain at the temple, a headache that wraps around the side of the head, pain behind the eye, nauseous headache.

Treatment (Mense and Simons 2001, 212). Abuse can be holding the muscle in a chronically shortened state, especially when that muscle is being contracted. This will turn a latent trigger point into an active one in no time! Holding the muscle in a chronically shortened position could be similar to what happens in the hamstrings when you sit for too long, slouch, and tuck your pelvis under. Abuse can be overusing the muscle, like working out too hard or carrying too many kids around the house and your arms and shoulders ache.

I would add that holding a muscle in a chronically lengthened position also activates trigger points, as I've witnessed many times over the years. We will explore this more in the last section of the book but for now, think about that nagging ache on the side of your neck. I often see that when one shoulder hangs lower than the other, the ache is often felt on the lower shoulder side. Stretching that is only going to make things worse. If you have that neck ache, and sometimes a headache on that same side of the head, take a look at yourself in the mirror. Does that shoulder drop lower than the other one?

SATELLITE TRIGGER POINTS

To make matters even more interesting, there is another type of trigger point, one that could be either latent or active. It's called a **satellite trigger point.** A satellite trigger point is one that develops in response to another trigger point somewhere else. Travell and Simons call the original trigger point the **main trigger point**. Their research found that often those main trigger points are followed by the development of trigger points either in the same muscle or in another muscle entirely (Travell, Simons, and Simons 1999). An example they give is trigger points in the trapezius muscle can be activated by trigger points in the triceps. Once they deactivated the trigger point in the triceps, there was no indication of a trigger point in the trapezius. They further explain that often the trigger point that is aching and causing a person to seek help is actually a satellite trigger point. And this is why sometimes you relieve a trigger point in one muscle and another muscle starts aching.

Ever had that experience? You seek relief from one thing and that gets better but then something else hurts, perhaps something you felt a long time ago? It may be that the pain from the original trigger point wasn't debilitating enough to prompt you to get help. But the pain from the satellite point was. This is why I always ask people to give me at least a few sessions to work with them because we have to address the whole system, not just one muscle or point.

Satellite trigger points can develop within the pain referral zone of the main trigger point, which I'll go into more detail about soon. In the example above, the trapezius can make your neck ache. Your neck muscles might feel very tender and rubbing your neck might feel like you are hitting trigger points, and you might be. It may be that a satellite trigger point has developed in the pain referral zone of the trapezius. But that satellite point in the neck is not the root cause of the issue. It's a result. Rubbing that spot will not fix the neck ache, as you may have experienced for yourself.

It's important to understand that trigger points have far-reaching effects. Trigger points in a muscle affect the muscles which create the same movements, called synergists, and the muscles that create the opposite movements, or antagonists. If one muscle holds a trigger point, or multiple points, then its mobility and strength are limited. This means that the other muscles that do the same job have to work harder. It also means that the muscles that do the opposite job will not be working to their optimum because their work is limited by the weakness of the first muscle. If one muscle is weak, the opposite muscle cannot lengthen to its full extent as it is pulled back by tension in the first muscle. Both become disabled over time. As well, some of those muscles might develop satellite trigger points in response to the main one. Whew!

Here's a common example that I see. If you sit for long periods of time, your hamstrings will develop trigger points. The hamstrings are now limited, and probably feel tight when you try to stretch them. The hamstrings bend the knee and lift the thigh behind you. The gluteus maximus is a synergist with the hamstrings, so now the gluteus maximus has to work harder when you walk due to the weakness in the hamstrings. The quadriceps on the front of the thigh are antagonists to the hamstrings and glute max. They straighten the knee, and one of the quads also lifts the thigh forward, called hip flexion. Now the quads are fighting the tension in the hamstrings and glute max. The quads are responsible for many cases of knee pain and knee buckling. Those knee issues may have all started with trigger points in the hamstrings. If you have knee pain and are looking at the knee joint for an explanation, you may not find it because the problem may be in the soft tissues and not in the joint itself.

One of the things that can be confusing to people in pain is that often the sensations generated by trigger points are not felt at the site of the trigger point itself. Yes, the point is tender to the touch, maybe *very painful* to the touch, but it can ache somewhere else. That's why the upper trapezius on the top of the shoulder can make your neck hurt and give you a headache.

This phenomenon is called a **trigger point pain referral**. Luckily, we have pain-referral maps that show us the trigger point and its associated pain. You saw that in the trapezius pain referral picture above. Butt pain might be coming from your outer hip, your lower back, or from a trigger point on the top rim of your pelvis. Weird right? But that's part of the magic, and seeming mystery, of trigger points. I want to demystify that for you. Let's look at pain referral patterns next.

CHAPTER 4

Trigger Point Symptoms

How do I know if I have trigger points? How do I know if the pain I am feeling is from a trigger point and not that something is damaged? What does trigger point pain feel like? And why does the trapezius muscle in my shoulder make my neck hurt and my head ache?

I asked one of my trigger-point instructors, Stew Wild, to tell us about trigger points. Stew works for MyoPain Seminars in Bethesda, Maryland, and runs his own trigger point therapy clinic, Myopain Solutions, in Dedham, Massachusetts. MyoPain Seminars is one of the leading organizations doing clinical research about trigger points as well as instructing trigger point dry needling and manual therapy. Stew is the only person they allow to teach manual trigger point therapy, meaning trigger point therapy done with the hands like I do with my clients. Dry-needling trigger point release is done with acupuncture needles directly into the points. Dry needling is typically done by a physical therapist.

Stew explained that "the trigger point gives rise to pretty much classic phenomenon, sensory motor (typically muscle pain and loss of mobility), and autonomic phenomenon (things like nausea, dizziness, sweaty palms, heart palpitations) that are very reproducible across different ethnicities and countries. They're reproducible throughout the world, and they're ubiquitous. Seldom do I ever find somebody *without* some kind of trigger point in their body." The fact that the symptoms are reproducible makes our job a little easier because Travell and Simons made us maps to follow.

Having a map means that if I am working with someone, no matter where in the world we are, if they have the pain referral pattern of the upper trapezius, neck pain, and a headache, sometimes with nausea, I can find and release that trigger point because I know where to look. I can follow the maps. My clients feel relief because that pain referral is the same for that trigger point location in everyone experiencing those symptoms. This is exactly the headache that Carmen had when she came to see me. Once she learned exactly where to go in her upper shoulder to release that trigger point, she stopped having headaches after an entire lifetime of headaches.

PAIN REFERRAL AND SHOULDER PAIN

Trigger points typically refer pain to other locations. Those pain referral areas overlap in multiple muscles. If you are feeling pain somewhere in your body, there could perhaps be a few different trigger points causing that pain. To get relief, you'd want to either see a therapist that understands trigger points or you'll want to follow the maps yourself and treat every muscle that could cause that pain until you find the right one. For instance, if you experience pain at the front of the shoulder, two muscles that can cause that pain are the pectoralis major in the chest or the infraspinatus muscle on the shoulder blade. For that front-of-the-shoulder pain, I have more often found it to be from the infraspinatus muscle. Here is a picture of the pain referral pattern for infraspinatus.

INFRASPINATUS PAIN REFERRAL PATTERN

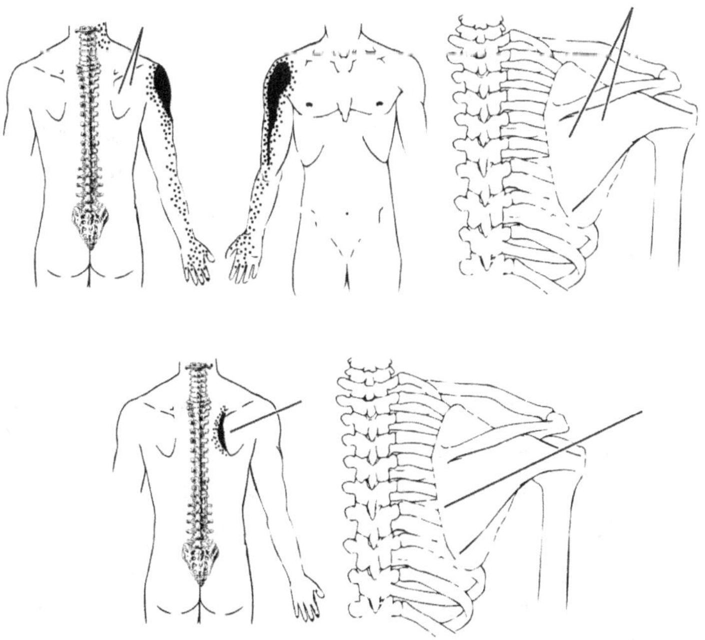

Infraspinatus pain referral pattern. Lines point to the location of trigger points. Shading indicates where pain or sensation is felt. Pain is often reported at the front of the shoulder and can go down the arm into the hand.

The infraspinatus lies on the outer surface of the shoulder blade in the upper back. It is a part of the rotator cuff. This muscle will externally rotate the arm, like when you reach behind you in the car to grab something from the back seat, and to help stabilize the shoulder joint. The infraspinatus often harbors a trigger point that refers to the front of the shoulder at the top and front of the arm. The infraspinatus can also cause aching along the biceps which can even radiate all the way down to your palm or down the back of the arm and to the back of the hand (Travell, Simons, and Simons 1999). All that from one little muscle! If you came to me with that issue and I didn't understand pain referral patterns, I wouldn't be able to help you. You'd leave with that same pain at the front of your shoulder. We may both blame the deltoid, which is a common mistake with infraspinatus trigger points. This is why so often non-trigger-point massage feels good and like the therapist is working in the correct area, but you don't feel relief afterward.

I've seen hundreds of people with shoulder pain that came to see me as a last resort before surgery. There was something inside telling them to not go through with the operation and to try trigger-point work first. Many of those clients left completely pain free, or well on their way, after just one session. I helped them because I followed the maps and understood where that pain was actually coming from and not where they felt it. I also treated the synergists and antagonists. With infraspinatus, I treat all the muscles of the rotator cuff and all the muscles that do the opposite action, namely the pectorals in the chest, the latissimus, and the teres major. I call those the Big Three and they are *always* a part of any shoulder problem.

The pecs, lats, and teres major all pull the arm down and rotate it inward, like when you slouch and round forward. The tiny infraspinatus lifts the arm and rotates it outward. If your pecs, lats, and teres major, the Big Three, are all loaded with trigger points and pulling strongly on the arm, you will have a very difficult time lifting your arm up over head to brush your hair, out to the side, or to reach behind you to grab something from the back seat. That one bit of information is often what people with shoulder issues are missing. Most of their healthcare team are not treating the Big Three; they are going right to the muscle with the pain and limitation. You have to address the underlying cause first, the main trigger points, or that problem won't go away. Later we'll talk about self-trigger-point release because you can do it yourself! Release your Big Three if you've got shoulder issues. I've seen folks get full range of motion restored in their shoulders in as little as thirty minutes after months, or years, of shoulder problems. Check out the shoulder playlist I created on my YouTube (@CatMatlock) channel. You can learn about the Big Three and how to release them there.

Again, trigger points are persistent and like to come back. That pain may not stay away after one session. (It definitely won't stay away if you go right back to slouching on the couch, shortening the Big Three.) It often takes several times of treating the area for the trigger point to go away, as well as attention to the other parts of the FreeBody System. This is why I teach clients to work on themselves and created my YouTube channel so they could follow videos. When you do self-trigger-point release regularly, you get out of pain much faster. My clients and students get themselves out of pain all the time. Then they also know how to keep it away.

Trigger points can sometimes refer pain really far away from the site of the point. One peculiar trigger point in a calf muscle named soleus can cause aching in the jaw. Stew and I talked about this one. He described a client he saw who is a glassblower who had broken her femur in an accident. She had plates and screws in her thigh, which led to the muscles in the thigh and leg to accumulate loads of trigger points. He said, "I could find that soleus point that went to her jaw every time she came because she's standing, leaning forward, and she's blowing glass all day." That position, coupled with the repercussions of the injury, had caused her to have trigger points in her calves. Luckily for her, when she went to see Stew for help with her injury, he also helped her jaw tension at the same time. That's the value of a good trigger point therapist.

Have you had some tension in your jaw you couldn't figure out? Spent hundreds or thousands of dollars on dentists, mouth guards, massage work to no avail? If yes, check your calves. There's more to it than that but it's not a bad place to check.

I asked Stew the reason for pain referrals. Why does that point on my shoulder blade in the back of my body cause pain at the front of my shoulder? He told me that inside the spinal cord, there are nerves that run alongside each other. Every part of your body has a nerve that it communicates with. The part of the body that a nerve talks to is known as a **receptive field**. Trigger points bombard the nerves with information and that information overflows and spills upward and downward into the nerves nearby. This causes those nerves nearby to react by creating pain and sensations in the places they communicate with, into their receptive fields. And that's a pain referral. It's an expansion of receptive fields.

The infraspinatus refers pain to the front of the shoulder because the nerves near the one that serve infraspinatus get bombarded with some of that sensory information. It's similar to an overflowing bucket. Those other nerves take up some of that overflow nerve stimulation from infraspinatus and send a message to the parts of the body they communicate with: the front of the shoulder. You then feel it in the front of your shoulder, or even down your biceps into your palm, so you think the problem is there. Or you might think it must be a nerve impingement because the pain covers such a large area. That's another common mistake that people with trigger points make. They think they have nerve impingement but it's actually just that one nerve, or multiple nerves, has taken on some of the overstimulation of the nerve near it in the spinal cord.

WHAT TRIGGER POINT PAIN FEELS LIKE IN YOUR BODY

So is all musculoskeletal pain from trigger points? The short answer is no. And again, as Clair and Amber Davies wrote in The *Trigger Point Therapy Workbook*, **at least 75 percent of all pain we feel** in our bodies was found to be a result of trigger points. That covers a *lot* of pain.

What does trigger point pain feel like? How can I know if it's coming from a trigger point or not? Clearly if you get injured and you're in lot of pain, go get checked out by a doctor to make sure you didn't tear anything or do some major tissue damage. Once you know that there's not been some serious damage, then you can go about dealing with the trigger points themselves, which are either fully causing the pain or contributing to it. Even with tissue damage, some of the pain is most likely coming from trigger points as well since muscles contract strongly in an attempt to protect the soft tissues, bones, and joints when there is an injury. That strong contraction is the perfect setup for trigger points.

Stew told me he listens for his clients to use the words "dull and achy." Travell and Simons use those words as well. The dull ache is a classic description of an active trigger point type of sensation. In my experience, it sometimes can be difficult to put your finger on exactly where it hurts. I've had clients say, "It's just in my shoulder somewhere." Other times, they might just point to the front of the shoulder and say, "Right there."

Clients have reported all kinds of sensations to me. As I noted above, Travell and Simons list numbness and tingling as a common trigger-point sensation. There is a trigger point in a lower back muscle called quadratus lumborum that can produce an electric-like stinging sensation at the sacro-iliac joint (SI joint). But electric and stinging are the exception, not the rule.

Weakness, as discussed earlier, is an indication of trigger points, and sometimes why folks come to me seeking help. I had one woman show up who couldn't lift her arms higher than just around shoulder height. She was in her early thirties and worked in a shipping department. She lifted and carried boxes all day long. She was looking into disability because she could barely lift her arms anymore. She was really scared and the doctors could find nothing wrong with her. The physical therapist she had seen gave her strengthening exercises, but that actually made her feel worse.

Travell and Simons speak to this. "The weakness and loss of work tolerance are often interpreted as an indication for increased exercise, but if this is attempted without inactivating the responsible trigger points, the exercise is likely to encourage and further ingrain substitution by other muscles and further weakening and deconditioning of the involved muscle." (Travell, Simons, and Simons 1999). This is exactly what was going on with this young woman. She got on my table and within thirty minutes, after almost a year of this disability, she had her full range of motion restored. She cried. We high fived. Hell yeah, trigger points are so cool! They can be a little tricky, but cool once you understand them.

Trigger points do not always send pain elsewhere. Sometimes the trigger point hurts right where the point is. Some places in the back near the spine do that. Do try rolling a ball or using a percussion massager, a.k.a. massage gun, on the area where you feel pain, just not directly on a bone. If that doesn't work, you'll want to look at trigger point pain referral maps to see where else to explore. A valuable resource I recommend is the website www.TriggerPoints.net. The website has an interactive map for those that don't know which muscle is causing their symptoms. You can go to the site, click on the body map on the area of your pain, and up pops a bunch of muscles which refer pain to that area. You can then hop over to my YouTube channel and learn how to release those muscles. On the channel, there are playlists for back pain, headaches, sciatica, and more. You will want to release the points in a variety of muscles and groups, not just the one causing you pain.

Here is a non-exhaustive list of symptoms that can be caused by trigger points.

- Tension headaches
- Some migraines, including those with aura and nausea
- Sciatica
- Low back pain, pain anywhere in the back
- Ilio-tibial band pain (along the outer thigh)
- Deep ache in the buttocks
- Jaw tension
- Toothache and tooth sensitivity to hot and cold
- Eye strain
- Ringing in the ears, tinnitus
- Shoulder pain
- Loss of range of motion at *any* joint
- Nerve pain
- Carpal tunnel syndrome
- Knee pain
- Knee buckling
- Hip flexor pain and tension
- Hip weakness
- Any joint weakness
- Groin pain
- Radiating numbness and tingling down the arms or legs
- Neck pain
- Shoulder pain, rotator cuff issues
- Sacro-iliac joint dysfunction
- Heel pain and plantar fasciitis

- Weakness in a muscle
- General fatigue
- Elbow pain
- Bursitis
- Trigger finger
- Rectal pain, vaginal pain, pelvic pain
- and so much more…

In the next chapter, I'm going to break down how trigger points can cause sciatica, because sciatica and lower back pain are my specialty. Even though I am going to share about sciatica specifically, the principles are the same with many painful conditions.

CHAPTER 5

Sciatica and Trigger Points

Got sciatica or know someone who suffers with it? Would you be surprised if I told you trigger points may be 100 percent the cause of those symptoms? Let's see how trigger points can cause sciatica. We'll explore other types of pain as we continue through this book together.

For about fifteen years, I suffered on and off with sciatica symptoms on my right side. I say "sciatica symptoms" because although I was told I had sciatica, I had what is called "false sciatica." It feels almost the same as true sciatica but it's not due to a compression on the sciatic nerve. It's actually due to trigger points which mimic sciatica symptoms. Many people who are chasing sciatica without relief are probably suffering from false sciatica.

When I had sciatica, sometimes the aching in my butt was so bad that I wanted to chop my butt off. When a flare-up occurred and things were bad, I would awaken in the middle of the night with a deep ache in my butt, which often traveled down my outer right thigh into my outer shin, sometimes to my foot. The ache in my hamstrings was relentless. My right hip was very weak, as I mentioned previously. I was diagnosed with sciatica and sought help from my yoga instructors, a physical therapist, chiropractors, and other massage professionals. Nearly all of those people blamed my piriformis (a muscle in the buttocks that goes from the sacrum to the hip joint) and I stretched that poor piriformis until I could barely walk. Stretching the piriformis never helped and often made things worse. If you have sciatica or piriformis syndrome, does this sound familiar?

I had some understanding of trigger points and decided to look more deeply into how trigger points could be causing my pain. It turns out that a muscle called gluteus minimus was the culprit. The symptoms from that little gluteus muscle on the side of the hip was named by Travell and Simons as "pseudo-sciatica." When I looked at the pain referral pattern, it matched exactly what I often felt in my body (Travell and Simons 1993).

I purchased *The Trigger Point Therapy Workbook* to learn how to release my points myself. Buy it today! I was hopeful that it would help me relieve my own trigger points, which it did, at least for a bit. I was able to locate those points in my gluteus minimus and when I lay on a ball on those points, it recreated the pain I often felt. I cried the first time I felt that. No one I'd seen had ever mentioned gluteus minimus and I felt like I had finally found the answer.

I rolled on that ball every day, and my symptoms would stop for a while but always came back, sometimes within hours. I was again frustrated and in pain. This is one reason why I believe some people want to discard trigger point release because it often does not work to just release the point that is giving you pain. Once I started expanding my self-trigger-point release work into the other muscles that do the same job as the gluteus minimus, such as gluteus medius, I had more relief. Then once I turned my attention to more muscles, including the antagonists in my inner thighs, I finally was able to get rid of my sciatica for good. I couldn't just work on the muscle that was actually causing my symptoms. I had to work on the synergists, muscles that do the same job, and the antagonists, muscles that do the opposite job, and then some other muscles as well. It's always a bit of a puzzle, but one that can be put together with the right understanding.

Here is a picture of the pain referral patterns of trigger points in the gluteus minimus (see image on page 52).

Look familiar? Deep ache in the butt which may ache down the outer thigh and may also make your hamstrings and calves ache. You see there's a difference between true sciatica, an actual compression on the sciatic nerve, and "false sciatica," which means you have all the symptoms of sciatica but it comes from trigger points. Most healthcare professionals don't know that there is a difference and you, like me, may have received a misdiagnosis. Something I wish I'd known is that neither true sciatica nor piriformis syndrome radiate down the outer thigh. But glute min does! Knowing that, and

GLUTEUS MINIMUS PAIN REFERRAL PATTERN

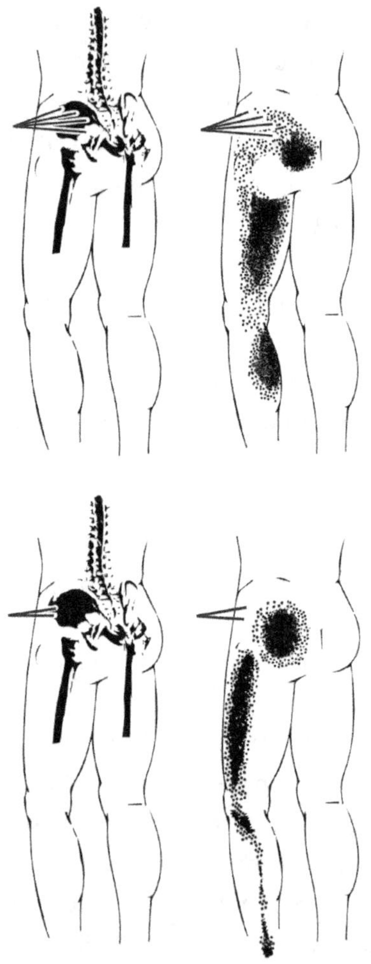

Gluteus minimus pain referral pattern.
Called "pseudo sciatica" by Travell and Simons.

applying all the principles in this system, will get you really far in your healing journey even if you have true sciatica. The sciatic nerve doesn't get compressed for no reason. Often that reason includes trigger points that you can release.

In my case, I was diagnosed with a "leg length discrepancy" and told my right leg was longer than my left. That's a terrible diagnosis because it made me believe I couldn't do anything about it. I mean, I couldn't change the length of my bones, right? But as I worked on my own body, I came to understand that it was actually a "hip height discrepancy," meaning my right hip was sitting higher than my left one. *That* is something we can work with because the muscles that pull the right hip up were full of trigger points. The muscles that pull the left hip down were, too. Once I started addressing the whole system, I was able to completely get rid of sciatica. Forever. I've helped many people get out of sciatica pain using the practices I discovered and developed to get rid of my own symptoms. It really works.

As I've said before, no muscle works in a vacuum and something like true or false sciatica is created by a bunch of muscles that aren't working properly. Even if you have a herniated disc, like I did, it begins with muscle issues. Discs don't just herniate on their own. And the disc herniation was *not* causing my pain. Not at all.

Trigger points were definitely a root cause of that herniation, though. The right hip was high because my quadratus lumborum, a muscle in the lower back that lifts the hip, was squashed short on the right side, which compressed the right side of my lumbar spine, squeezing the disc out to the left.

The disc herniated to the left. My symptoms were on the right. The pain I felt was from trigger points in a hip muscle on the right, which was stuck too long. Since the right side of my pelvis was high and the glute min attaches onto it, the glute min was being pulled long and it was trying to pull my hip back down. Trigger points in the glute min became activated over time and caused me that terrible pain.

Here are the pain referral patterns for the quadratus lumborum muscle in the low back. You can see this muscle attaches along the lumbar spine from the top rim of the pelvis to the lowest rib. When the muscle contracts, it draws the end points toward each other. It draws the pelvis and the rib closer together, effectively hiking up that hip. Trigger points in my quadratus lumborum muscle caused some of my butt pain and set the stage for my sciatica symptoms.

QUADRATUS LUMBORUM PAIN REFERRAL PATTERN: DEEP LAYERS

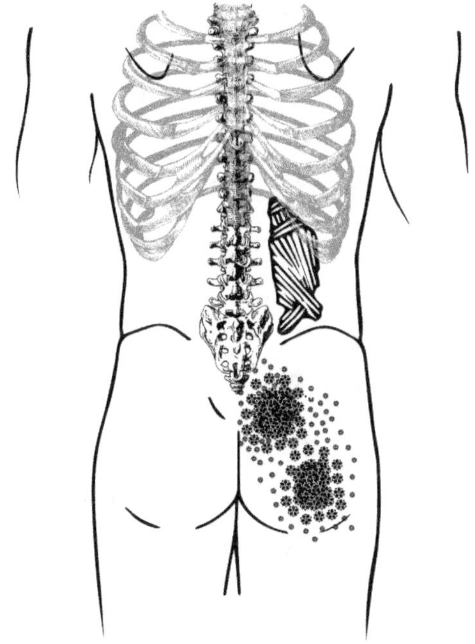

Deep quadratus lumborum trigger points cause a deep ache in the buttocks and/or the sacroiliac joint. This pain sometimes has a lightning-like quality and literally bring you to your knees. Crawling can feel better than walking.

QUADRATUS LUMBORUM PAIN REFERRAL PATTERN: SUPERFICIAL LAYERS

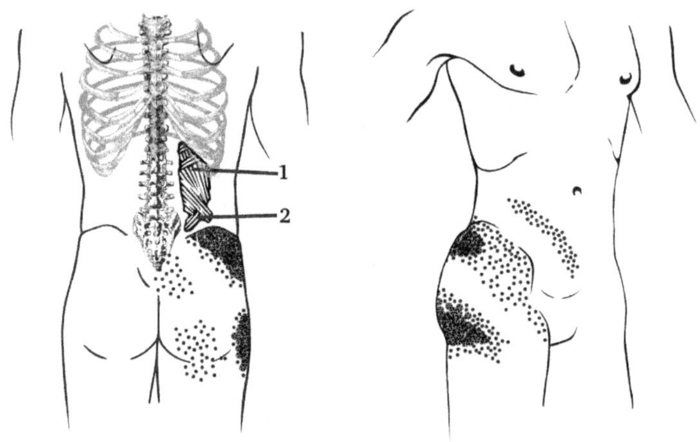

Superficial quadratus lumborum trigger points can cause
an ache across the top of the hip joint, on the lower part of
the outside of the hip, and an ache that wraps around
the side of the belly, even inside the pelvis.

CHAPTER 6

Trigger Points, Aging, and Old Injuries

―――

AGING

We have been programmed to believe that aging must be painful. We are taught to expect arthritis, joint dysfunction, and nagging pain that gets worse over time. Listen to any ads targeted to older populations and you will realize how pervasive this belief has become. While that does happen for some people, and aging certainly does affect our bodies, I believe you can age much more gracefully than you might currently believe is possible.

So far in this book you have learned that trigger points can cause weakness, pain, and loss of mobility. Doesn't that sound like a picture of aging? Trigger points can make your joints hurt through pain referral patterns. They also affect how the muscles pull on those joints, perhaps creating a distortion of that joint, setting up the conditions for bone spurs and arthritis. Since trigger points reduce the range of motion at a joint, all the muscles that act on that joint will be affected and all of them may become weaker and develop painful trigger points.

Trigger points are persistent and like to stick around. Remember Carmen with the headaches? 70 years of pain because those trigger points in her trapezius didn't go away on their own. Since nearly everyone is harboring trigger points somewhere in their bodies, those points may be affecting your muscles, tissues, and joints for a long time without you ever being aware of it. We tend to only notice the active trigger points because they *actively* cause pain. Once the pain goes away, we stop thinking about them. What may have happened, though, is that the trigger points shifted from the active to the latent phase. They no longer cause pain but they still limit mobility and affect a host of other muscles. Over time, all of those muscles become less capable of doing their work. You feel older, weaker, and don't get up from the couch as easily at the end of the movie.

TENSIONAL RECIPES FROM OLD INJURIES

When you experience an injury, say a car accident for example, your muscles contract strongly to protect your spine and soft tissues, such as muscles, ligaments, and tendons, from being torn. In the car accident example, the muscles that stabilize the spine in the neck and lower back engage and often get stuck with trigger points. Have you ever had a car wreck? Perhaps your neck was really stiff for a while afterward. Or perhaps your lower back or hips ached for a while. As your body settles and leaves the initial phase of protection, the active trigger points may downgrade to the latent phase, but they are still in there.

After that accident, your neck may have felt stiff more often and turning your head to the side was more challenging. You may have felt more back pain that came and went, as the trigger points went up and down from latent to active to latent again. Perhaps now you slip and grab onto something to catch your fall, your neck muscles engage to protect your spine, and the same symptoms you experienced after the accident come back full force.

I recall one man who, when he came to see me for the first time, was literally standing sideways. His hips were where they were supposed to be but his torso was way over to the right. He had been playing with his daughter and her friends on a trampoline and didn't feel any pain or any problem at the time. Everything seemed fine. The next day he awoke with terrible pain in his back and couldn't stand upright, just kind of sideways. He told me of an old injury he'd had over twenty years prior in which he fell off a ladder. After the ladder injury, he had ended up exactly as he was then, sideways and in pain.

His body had pulled that old tensional recipe card to protect him. It ignited the same spots as it had years before. This was easy to do because his trigger points hadn't actually gone away, just gone latent. Those trigger points were in there, ready to activate, and so they did. This is a common reason that I see folks get into trouble with old injuries. It is not that they have tissue damage, they just have tons of latent trigger points that can, and will, be activated with a slip, fall, or other sudden jolt. One of my clients reached out to me to request an appointment because his sciatica had returned with a vengeance. When I asked him what happened he said, "I was just putting on my underwear, my toe got stuck, and I fell."

But this doesn't need to happen. You can regularly attend to your body, release your active and latent trigger points, and not have to worry about that injury coming back because the points that would do that no longer exist. And if it does come back, you can take care of it right away. You don't get stuck in that same pain. No worry. No pain. No problem.

I said it before and I'll repeat it here: I feel better in my fifties than I did in my twenties. I no longer worry about sciatica or back pain. If I do get injured, and you'll hear more about a back injury I had last year, I can take care of it. I want you to feel that kind of confidence. Later I will teach you how to release your own trigger points. For now, we must continue laying the foundation of the FreeBody System by moving our attention from the muscles themselves into the wrapper around them: the fascia.

PART 2

FASCIA

CHAPTER 7

The Wonderful Web of Fascia

With the explosion of research on fascia in the last twenty years, new doors have flown wide open to help us understand more about our bodies and the pain we feel. Fascia envelops every muscle and, in fact, every single thing in your body. It encapsulates each individual muscle cell, or fiber, and also each muscle as a whole. It wraps your organs, brain, bones, nerves, and everything in between. Fascia is a continuous unifying web of tissue.

What you'll discover in this section is that fascia is kind of a master tissue that guides communication between all our systems. It shapes every other system and can change its shape and structure on demand. Inflammation happens in the fascia. Fascia is the tissue that gets dehydrated, that gets stuck, and that traps inflammation and pain. Let's dive in and explore this extraordinary thing called fascia!

CHAPTER 8

What Is Fascia?

Throughout your body, there is a magical and responsive scaffolding-of-sorts tissue called fascia. Fascia is a shape shifter, changing itself based on the needs of the body in any given situation or location. Sometimes it connects things, sometimes it acts as support, sometimes a separator, sometimes a semiconductor of electrical charges. It is also the host for many sensory receptors, nerve endings that are taking in information and sending signals to the brain, including pain receptors. We cannot explore pain without exploring fascia.

Familiar forms of fascia are tendons, ligaments, and bands such as the ilio-tibial band, which runs from the top of the hip bone (the ilium) to below the knee on the tibia. For most of anatomy science history, fascia was considered simply structural support, linking muscles and bones, and helping muscles to transmit force for movement. But what is emerging is that fascia is actually far more than that and is quite related to the aches and pains we feel.

Take Delayed Onset Muscle Soreness (DOMS) for example. You know that sore feeling that happens when you work out harder than usual, or decide that you are going to do fifty sit-ups one day when you haven't done sit-ups for twenty years? You're fine for a day or so, but then you get out of bed and your abs are really *really* sore. That's a classic example of DOMS. We always thought that was coming from the muscles, hence the name. Well, it turns out that the soreness you feel is actually coming from the fascia around the muscle, which wraps the muscle like a bag (Wilke and Behringer 2021). Heads up that DOMS has nothing to do with lactic acid! Everyone thought that lactic acid buildup was the cause. That myth was debunked in 1980 (Brooks and Gaesser 1980). That soreness appears to come from the fascia.

So what is this fascia anyway? Why does it cause me to feel pain? Where is it in the body and how can I work with it to feel better?

To understand the answers to these questions, let's take a look inside our extraordinary bodies and see what the heck fascia is, what it does, and how it changes. Sometimes fascia changes for the good and sometimes, well, it just might be the answer to why you have that backache.

WHAT IS FASCIA?

There is actually not a clear direct answer to this question because our understanding of fascia is still developing. And fascia is not one thing. Fascia is the white stuff between all your other stuff that usually ended up in the waste bin during dissections. For a long time, much of the fascia was cut away and tossed out as it was not considered to be important. Only the prominent fascial structures were left to look at and explore, like tendons and ligaments. That is until recently when researchers began to wonder if maybe that stuff they were throwing away actually had some answers they were seeking.

Fascia comes in many shapes, sizes, and structural components. It plays multiple roles in keeping us healthy and warning us when things go awry. Fascia is a type of connective tissue. There are only four types of tissues in the body. Those four types of tissues are neural, epithelial, muscular, and connective tissue. Neural means anything in the nervous system, like nerves and the parts of the brain. Epithelial tissues are skin and the lining inside your organs. Muscular tissue is, well, the muscles, and there are two types of those: skeletal muscle tissues like the biceps and hamstrings, and smooth muscle tissues that are in organs such as those that pump the heart and those in the intestines that contract to move poop through.

Everything else is connective tissue. Every connective tissue has some combination of cells and/or fibers and the fluid those cells live in, called a matrix. Types of connective tissue change form depending on factors such as what kinds and ratios of fibers it contains and what's inside that fluid matrix. Blood is a connective tissue with no fibers. Bones are a connective tissue whose matrix is mostly calcium and minerals. Tendons are a connective tissue that have some collagen, the strongest and most abundant fiber in the body, and some elastin, which makes them flexible. Ligaments have fewer elastic fibers and more collagen, so they are tougher and stronger than tendons. There are many variations of connective tissues too numerous to mention and not relevant to our discussion here.

Fascia is a kind of connective tissue that is often characterized by its "sheet-like" quality, yet fascia also changes its form and texture depending on the role it plays wherever it is located. There are broad sheets of fascia that travel from the back of your pelvis up to the ribcage, called the thoracolumbar fascia. We're going to talk more about that important area later, because it is key in understanding chronic lower back pain. The ilio-tibial band along the outer thigh is a thick band of fascia that connects the outer pelvis to the outer knee, stabilizing the two in movement.

Fascial straps are found everywhere throughout the body, tacking things down and guiding other structures. The roof of the carpal tunnel is a band of fascia, called the wrist flexor retinaculum or the transverse carpal ligament. That's the part they cut during carpal tunnel surgery with the intention to free the tendons beneath it. Those tendons, nine in all that pass through the tunnel, get jacked up or "inflamed," compressing the median nerve, which causes the symptoms of carpal tunnel syndrome. The surgery is meant to relieve that pressure, and it often works, yet now you've got scar tissue from the surgery. I have found that releasing the trigger points in those muscles, and freeing the fascia in the area, eases the tendons and relieves the pressure and carpal tunnel syndrome symptoms. Sometimes within about half an hour. But I digress.

Every structure in your body is wrapped in a fascial bag, or fascial envelope. If you removed the fascial bag from your hamstrings, they would turn into a pile of fiber-y goo. Fascia gives shape and structure to everything else in your body. Fascia guides, separates, connects, and communicates with every other system in your body. If you removed every other kind of cell but left the fascia, you'd have a perfectly shaped picture of essentially your entire form (Myers 2001).

Since fascia changes its shape and structure, even anatomists have had a hard time pinpointing what fascia actually is and which structures and substances to call fascia. All seem to agree that fascia is a combination of fibers, basically many types of collagen and elastin, fibroblasts that make those fibers, and the liquid bath matrix, a.k.a. ground substance, which serves multiple functions. The ground substance hosts immune cells such as lymphocytes and fibroblasts, as well as a host of other cell messengers like mast cells, which produce histamine. We will explore this ground substance matrix later on because it has a lot to do with pain and inflammation.

The fascial system is an intricate web that connects every single cell of the body to every other cell. Fascia is continuous throughout the entire body, kind of like a bodysuit that holds everything inside you. We are more one organism, one fascial bodysuit, with various pockets of muscles, organs, and nerves than with distinct and separate features. Everything is connected to everything else via fascia.

There is new and exciting research on the role fascia plays in the loss of mobility, pain, and inflammation. Let's take a look.

CHAPTER 9

Fascia and Lower Back Pain

Are you one of the millions of people suffering with pain in your lower back? Perhaps you've tried a bunch of things and nothing seems to quite get rid of it? Do you feel tense, tight, restricted, and perhaps a bit worried? If yes, then this chapter is especially important for you. If you don't have back pain currently, good for you! You still need to read this because back pain is so very common, and there's new understanding that will keep you from going down that dark road.

One of my original massage instructors, Paul Davenport, said at the Florida School of Massage in 1992, "Your body responds to the demands you put on it." Those demands are how much you move, what kinds of movements you do, how you sit and stand, and generally, how you live in your body. It seems that the fascia not only responds to your demands, it reshapes itself based on what you are telling it through those actions. For instance, every muscle is wrapped in a fascial bag, called the perimysium. When you build strength in a muscle, this sends a message to the perimysium to get thicker, and so it does. The fascia responds and everything is fine. Then when you allow the muscles to get weaker, that fascial bag responds by getting thinner (Schleip 2017, 73). A thinner fascial bag will tear more easily, resulting in inflammation and pain. This is especially important when understanding back pain.

In very recent years, researchers have been turning their attention away from muscular and spinal disc causes of a variety of pain syndromes such as lower back pain and looking instead to fascia. Many back pain syndromes could not be explained via muscular causes, or disc injuries and deterioration. As a matter of fact, back in 1994, studies proved that many healthy, pain-free individuals were found to have a variety of bulging and altered discs. But no pain! The researchers determined that this was *so often the case*, as seen on MRIs, that "the discovery by MRI of bulges or protrusions in people with lower back pain may frequently be coincidental" (Jensen et al. 1994).

Some back pain couldn't be explained by the muscles or the discs because the pain wasn't coming from them at all.

Both muscle tissues and fascial tissues contribute to the aches and pains we feel. Muscles and fascia are inseparable and work together, each having its own connection to tension and pain. Jan Dommerholt, the US's leading expert and clinical researcher on trigger points, explains that the perimysium (the fascial bag around a muscle) is "capable of increasing muscle stiffness, which is a common finding in myofascial pain" (Dommerholt 2012, 301). That makes sense, right? When you hurt, you often feel tight. Much of that tight feeling is coming from the fascia and not the muscle itself.

LOWER BACK PAIN AND FASCIA

The World Health Organization reported in July 2022 that "Musculoskeletal conditions are the leading contributor to disability worldwide, with *low back pain* being the single leading cause of disability in 160 countries" (WHO 2022). Globally there is great need for more understanding of lower back pain. Turns out, fascia is a key component.

Robert Schleip is a global leader in fascia research. He worked as a psychologist, then a fascia bodyworker through the Rolf Institute, then received his PhD in biology and fascia. Dr. Schleip was the impetus for the first International Fascia Research Congress, which meets every two to three years to share information and clinical studies on fascia. His work has been crucial in furthering our understanding of this tissue.

In his book *Fascial Fitness,* Dr. Schleip explains that the lumbar fascia, the fascia in the lower back, is shown to have become "matted" and bound up in people with lower back pain. The patients they studied with back pain have a fascia that is "clearly thickened in the lower back region; and it does not slide as freely as it does in healthy persons." This thickening of the fascia then affects the way the person walks, affecting their gait. Those changes in gait and loss of free mobility can lead to pain (Schleip 2017).

Let's get some clarity on what this lumbar fascia is. Lumbar is the term for the lower back. The lumbar spine is the part of the spine in the lower back. The lumbar fascia, also known as the thoracolumbar fascia (TLF) consists of two layers of broad, thick sheets of fascia. "Thoraco" indicates that it attaches up on the thorax, or ribcage. The TLF consists of two layers of *dense* connective tissue that begins on the pelvis and rises up across the lower back and into the lower rib area. These layers are meant to slide on each other. This fascia provides support and structure in the lower back, transmitting much of the force from our movements when we stand upright. It's kind of like a natural corset or weight-lifting belt. Can you see that in the picture below? It is this area that takes the load of the upper body and transfers that weight to the lower limbs, from the lumbar spine across the sacro-iliac joints to be distributed to the legs below (Vleeming 2012, 41). Walking is actually quite a mechanical wonder! And fully supported by the TLF.

The TLF is rich with muscular attachments. Low back muscles, the glutes, the muscles on the sides of your abdomen, and the trapezius (which goes all the way to the base of your skull) all weave themselves into the TLF. The strong fabric of the TLF is transmitting the forces of all of these muscles as we move. *Wow!*

This is important because all of those muscles are each pulling on this fabric of the TLF. Imagine if you have some dysfunction in your hip, like a weakness in one hip or perhaps aching in your hip after a long walk or run. Perhaps you have a "hip height inequality" and your pelvis is not level.

THORACOLUMBAR FASCIA

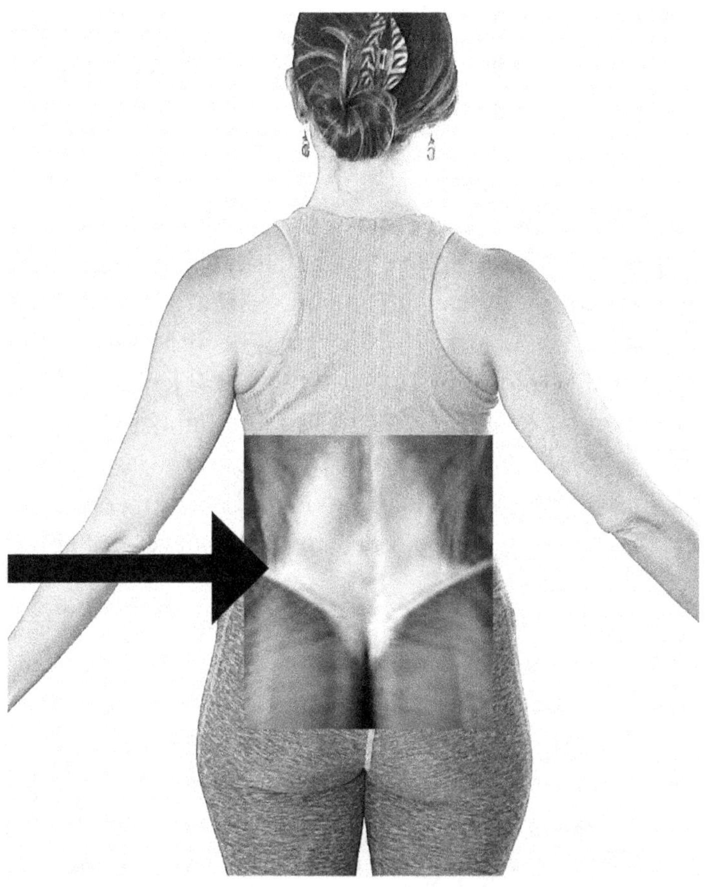

The thoracolumbar fascia, TLF, is always involved with lower back pain.

The muscles that produce those symptoms and conditions are directly pulling on the TLF and communicating through it. If some of the muscles that connect into the TLF are not fully functional, that may affect all the other muscles which attach into and communicate through this fascia. And that is a lot of muscles, even all the way up to the base of your skull.

Thinking of it in this way, I can see even more clearly how the lower back is susceptible to aches, pains, and dysfunction. When I had sciatica, my right hip was chronically high. That higher hip would always distort the TLF and affect all the muscles that attach into it. My left hip was low, so my left outer hip muscles were always short and tight, and pulling on the TLF. My TLF was crooked, felt tight, and it hurt. This is another reason why focusing on and releasing one muscle doesn't work. Musculoskeletal pain is never just about one thing.

Schleip found that not only are these fascial layers thicker in people with lower back pain, but they don't glide well. In many, they have become adhered to each other. That means that this flexible dense fabric has become rigid and less capable of movement in people with low back pain (Schleip 2017). If you have lower back pain, you probably feel "tight" in that area. This could be due to a rigid TLF.

Schleip also explains that the lumbar fascia is richly innervated with nociceptors, or pain receptors. Having a lot of pain receptors in one area means that the area will be more susceptible to pain. Dr. Schleip, in a podcast interview published by the Academy of Clinical Massage, said, "fascia is there for pain-related body perception" (2021). That means fascia is partly, and seemingly highly, concerned with pain awareness throughout the whole body. Schleip's studies have shown that the lumbar fascia is very richly innervated with the nerve endings that detect pain.

The more pain receptors an area has, the more pain it is capable of producing. What that may mean is that back pain as the leading musculoskeletal pain worldwide may partly be a result of the fact that our lower backs are more *capable* of experiencing pain than other areas of the body. This makes me think of the early trigger point explorations of Travell and Simons and how they listed the lower back muscles as **target muscles**. Target muscles are muscles in the body that are painful when there are trigger points in a variety of muscles (Travell, Simons, and Simons 1999). Basically, several different muscles refer pain into the lower back. Perhaps some of the pain there is actually a result of thickening in the lumbar fascia, stimulating its pain receptors and not in the muscles.

Whoa. Pause a moment and take that in. This is groundbreaking understanding for sufferers of lower back pain. The pain in your lower back may be a result of that area having more pain receptors, increasing the chances of pain to be felt there. And it likely includes a thick and matted TLF, which can be softened and freed. And don't worry, I will give you some understanding of the latest techniques available to affect the lumbar fascia and reduce that experience of pain. But first there's more to understand.

INFLAMMATION AND PAIN RECEPTORS

Let's consider inflammation for a moment. Inflammation occurs in fascia. Remember I mentioned ground substance earlier and said we'd get back to it? Ground substance is the fluid in fascia, that liquid matrix. Something that's really cool about ground substance is that it has nearly exactly the same ratios of salts as are in ocean water (Meert 2012, 177). We are all walking around carrying a little ocean within us, our cells swimming in it throughout our entire bodies.

It is within this fluid that the cells which trigger inflammation reside. When a body has an inflammatory response, that happens in the fascia. Fascia inflames. When we have an injury, the protective mechanism of inflammation gets triggered. An interesting study that was done on the lumbar fascia in rats found that, apparently as a result of manufactured inflammation, the number of pain receptors, the nociceptors, significantly increased in the fascia (Hoheisel, Rosner, and Mense 2015).

That may mean that when a part of the body is inflamed, that area spontaneously becomes more populated with pain receptors. Pain is a protective mechanism. So is inflammation. The body steps up its protective mechanisms when there is the danger of injury or invasion. The TLF already has a high number of pain receptors and then the body creates more there as a response to the inflammation. Our bodies are amazing! And of course, that can cause you more pain.

Here is how all of that could translate to you and lower back pain. Let's say you pick something up that's pretty heavy, such as a child that is sick. You lift up a sick child because you have to get them to the bathroom at 2 a.m. to go throw up. If you've ever done this, you know how important it is to move as fast as possible! You lean over to grab the child, scoop them up, stand up, and twist to run toward the door. Except... *Ouch*! If the muscles in your back are a little weak, their fascial bag will be a little thinner than it should be. That thin fascial bag is prone to tear. That tear triggers an inflammatory response so the tissue can heal. So now you've got this little bit of inflammation in your back. If that inflammation goes away quickly once the torn tissue is repaired, you're good. But if it doesn't, for a number of factors, and you get stuck in chronic inflammation, then the thicker lumbar fascia, the TLF, actually gets thicker.

The layers of fascia can be a little confusing sometimes. So for clarity, the muscle is wrapped in a thinner envelope: its fascial bag. When muscles weaken, their fascial bag gets thinner and more prone to tears. The TLF lies over those thinner bags. The TLF in people with lower back pain is thicker. So you have this thick and limited dense layer on top of thinner weaker muscle fascial bags. There is the potential for them to get stuck together and trap inflammation. During an inflammatory response, the TLF becomes more rigid. And to make matters worse, the number of pain receptors within that lumbar fascia actually increases! So now your lower back has more pain receptors, which heightens your sensation of pain in your lower back. Gah!

You may start to walk a little funny, perhaps not fully moving the way you usually do. Your fascia responds to that change by, perhaps, thickening the lumbar fascia even more. That fascial thickening will further limit your movement. The muscles aren't moving to their fullest potential, so they weaken. This triggers the muscular fascial bags, the perimysium, to get thinner, which makes them more prone to injury. If those bags tear, more inflammation ensues. An increase of inflammation triggers an increase in the number of pain receptors...and increase the experience of pain. All of this is happening while your muscles are getting trigger points, which may produce more pain, further weaken the area, and further limit the range of motion. This is a common scenario for people with chronic lower back pain. But it doesn't have to be the end of the story. The FreeBody method will give you tools to work with the trigger points and the fascia both, as I'll expound upon soon.

Emerging research on fascia is exciting and more comes out every day. This research helps us understand more about our bodies and the pains we feel. Let's take a deeper look at the extraordinary capacity for fascia to mold itself based on how we live in our bodies and take one more look at ground substance.

CHAPTER 10

The Magical Morphing Jell-O Inside You

As a child in the '70s, I grew up eating that mystical dessert called Jell-O. My mom would heat up some sugary water and add the packet full of gelatin, artificial flavoring, and artificial colors, you know, before anyone started talking about the health effects of artificial flavorings and colors. It tasted so good! I would help her stir the magic mixture in the pot on the stove. She'd open up a can of fruit cocktail, drain it, and dump it into a mold, and I'd pour the liquid Jell-O into it. The Jell-O mix was warm and *slickery*: slick and slippery at the same time. (Yes, that's my made up word. It works!) We'd put the mold in the fridge to become solid for our dessert, topped with whipped cream of course. Who's with me on this memory? Magic, right? Every once in a while, I'd open the fridge and shake that mold to see how solid it had gotten, to see how much it moved. My mom would yell, "Leave it alone! It has to set!" For the Jell-O to set, it had to be still and it had to be cold. I wanted to observe the magic as it happened.

It turns out this type of gelatinous goo fills your entire body. It transfers force, keeps things gliding around inside so they don't get stuck and tear, keeps things nourished, removes waste, offers support for repair, and basically supports all your life processes within you.

Gelatin that you eat comes from the connective tissue of animals, usually hoofed animals such as pigs and horses. You can boil down their skin, tendons, and bones and voila, you've got gelatinous goo. If you make bone broth, you know what I'm talking about. You want that broth to get thick and goopy in the fridge. You essentially make Jell-O from scratch, sans the sugar, red coloring, and artificial cherry flavor.

That same substance is in your own body. This is the ground substance. On the micro level, it's called the extra cellular matrix, the ECM. It's the viscous (slickery) substance that surrounds cells everywhere. It is into this matrix that cells dump their waste products and through which they ask the matrix for repair and support. On the macro level, Gil Hedley calls it **perifascia**, the fascia that surrounds everything. Ground substance is the liquid matrix inside the perifascia. Gil Hedley is an anatomist I've followed for about fifteen years. He offers human dissection courses and operates his website, www.GilHedley.com, where his research and courses are hosted. He calls those of us who geek out on exploring the body *Somanauts*. If, like mine, your idea of a fun afternoon is watching people look at dissected bodies and talk about how cool they are, I highly recommend you join his membership program. I love it! And I learn so much.

I had the good fortune to interview Gil Hedley. Gil describes our fascial bags and sheets, such as tendons, as "spaghetti in Jell-O," the Jell-O being the perifascia. He said, "The deep fascia (those sheets) are embedded in it. Perifascia is a membranous substance in which the dense fibrous fascia are embedded and that [perifascia] makes it slippery on either side of that tissue so that the deep fascia, [tendon] being anchored to bone and continuous with it...can have its movement and stability-providing function, while the perifascia can provide the connection and the interface which allows for play with other tissues in relationship to the deep fascia."

In the dissection lab, he can see the structures, the spaghetti, held inside the Jell-O. He can cut a layer and those deep fascia structures, like tendons and ligaments and fascial bags, are surrounded completely by the Jell-O. As he cleans off the Jell-O and removes spaghetti, he finds more Jell-O underneath. He made the point that the Jell-O perifascia and the deep fascia sheets are continuous with one another. They appear distinct, as a tendon appears distinct from the bone it attaches into. But if you look closely, the tendon becomes continuous with the periosteum, the fascial bag around the bone. They merge together and you cannot really tell where one ends and one begins. The same is true with the perifascia and the other forms of fascia that live inside of it.

This is the absolute magic of fascia! It changes its structure depending on the task at hand, like the tendon becoming the wrapper around the bone. In ligaments there is just a little bit of liquidy goo inside because ligaments need to be tough, fibrous, and strong. The discs in your spine need to absorb much more shock and move a lot, so they are more slickery goo and less fiber. The discs have more ground substance, more liquid matrix.

If we didn't have this perifascia, we would be dry inside, and our organs and tissues would just stick together. Our organs need to be able to move as we move, or their fascial bags would tear. The perifascia keeps your liver from tearing open and spilling out when you go for a run. Our muscles need to be able to slide on one another to allow for movement, so they are surrounded by perifascia. Perifascia is the slickery stuff that allows for them to slide. Perifascia is the hydrous matrix that should exist between the layers of your thoracolumbar fascia, so those sheets of fascia can slide on each other. Without it, as mentioned earlier, those layers get stuck and the TLF gets thick, limiting your movement, trapping inflammation, and perhaps driving lower back pain.

Frans Van den Berg, in his chapter in a book titled *Fascia: The Tensional Network of the Human Body*, explains that within the ECM there must be enough liquid, enough ground substance, to keep the fibers within it from sticking together. His research shows that ground substance is found between collagen fibers and that fluid reduces friction and keeps the collagen fibers from pathologically binding to each other when they should stay separated. When the fluid is reduced, this essential space between fibers diminishes and the collagen fibers get stuck together, movement is limited, and pain may result (Van den Berg 2012, 150). It's exactly the same as between the larger structures, like the layers of the TLF. Without enough fluid, the layers stick together. On a micro level, without enough fluid, the fibers stick together. This is why dehydration is such a bad thing. Things get stuck on the micro and the macro level.

Collagen is strong and sticky. It drives the connective part of connective tissue. It's the one holding the potluck and bringing everyone together for a group hug. Not only does connective tissue unite everything inside our bodies simply by being everywhere, it also physically binds to other connective tissues when the tissues get dehydrated. Collagen binds. It can also be produced on demand. Let's look at how that happens.

FASCIAL BAGS

Within the fascial bags that wrap your muscles, collagen production can increase, thickening the walls around the muscles. Recall that the envelope surrounding an entire muscle is called the **perimysium**. If you opened up that bag and looked inside, you would see bundles of fibers, **fascicles**, wrapped together in their own little fascial bags called **epimysium**. If you opened up those fascicles, you'd find that every single muscle fiber has its own wrapper of fascia, the **endomysium**. Yet again, fascia compartmentalizes and connects every structure. If you are a bodyworker or massage therapist, you are never just working with muscles. You are always, without exception, working with fascia. They are inseparable.

Once thought to be inert, it turns out that fascia is actually quite responsive to stressors and forces put upon it through movement. For instance, I mentioned earlier that Schleip pointed out that in folks suffering with lower back pain, the perimysium around their lower back muscles had gotten thin, making it prone to tears and injury. When you use a muscle, that action pulls on the fascia, which stimulates the fascial bag to become thicker. This allows it to withstand and direct the force of the muscle that pulls on it. When you don't use your muscles, this makes the fascia thinner. The stronger the muscle, the more pull there is on the fascia, the more collagen is produced, the thicker it's fascial bag. The fascia is directing the force of the muscles (Schleip 2017). This means it must be thick enough to withstand the force of the muscle pulling on it, so this kind of thickening is a good thing. It's when the fluid matrix, or the perifascia, between the layers get too low that they get stuck, which results in an undesirable thickening. I know, it's a lot to take in, but hang in there because it's important to understand these concepts if you want to feel free in your body. You know, FreeBody.

As collagen is the strongest fiber in the body, the fascia responds to rigorous mechanical demands, like strength training, by creating more collagen. This is how the fascial bag gets thicker. Collagen has the tensile strength of steel, as is commonly known in the anatomy world. With more collagen in the fascial web, that web becomes stronger and more capable of withstanding force. When we use our muscles, we generate more collagen to thicken their fascial bags so they can withstand the force exerted by the muscle itself. Brilliant! If you get weaker, that collagen is reabsorbed and the fascial bag gets thinner again.

We want to keep our fascial bags thick enough to withstand the forces of movement by training over time. This is why someone with weak back muscles and thin fascial bags experiences tears in those bags when they do something sudden and burdensome, like lifting a sick child and turning suddenly at the same time. You need to keep your muscles strong and your fascia strong enough to support them because you never know when your kid is going to throw up.

On the other side of that coin, muscular training can also be done too quickly and forcefully, without regard to its dynamically responsive fascial counterpart. If you overtrain your muscles too quickly, without caring for your fascia properly, your fascia will likely tear. When training your muscles, it's a good idea to train your fascia along with them, which requires a different kind of attention. Fascia training requires taking enough time to systematically build strength in the muscle while allowing the fascia to integrate the new strength. You need to rest muscles on off days, not pushing them every day, to allow the fascia to generate collagen and get thicker. You also need to keep your fascia hydrated, which I will cover in the sections on movement and self-myofascial release later in the book. There are also videos on the website to help you. I got you!

GROUND SUBSTANCE AND EXTRACELLULAR MATRIX

Ground substance is in every form of fascia. Ground substance is the liquid slickery substance into which cells dump their waste, or metabolites. That liquid, and what's inside it, changes due to which cells it supports, depending on the needs of the cell. Literally every cell in the body is supported by the ground substance fluid around it. Through this substance, communication between systems occurs, cellular waste is processed, and immune function occurs, among other things.

The ECM is around all your cells, sort of like little viscous ponds, supporting essential processes for those cells like removing waste and bringing nutrients (Van den Berg 2012, 165.) When you link all of these fluid areas together, you get what Gil Hedley calls perifascia. Every system is connected, and kept critically apart, by perifascia. Remember that when the fluid in the perifascia gets low, things stick together.

Since every system lives in a bath of ground substance, every system is effected by fascial thickening and dehydration. Consider this for a moment. Cells are dumping their waste into the ECM to be processed. The perifascia must be hydrated with enough ground substance to move that waste along. **Mast cells** also live in the perifascia; actually, they are nearly everywhere in the body except the cornea of the eye and the central nervous system and must have liquid to travel through (Krystel-Whittemore et al. 2016). Mast cells are most famous for excreting histamine, a chemical messenger to alert the presence of danger perhaps in the form of an allergen. That is one of their jobs. Triggering an inflammatory response is another.

Mast cells actually keep tabs on a host of immunological processes (Krystel-Whittemore et al. 2016). Just like the cellular waste which needs liquid to move through, the mast cells (and a host of other cells to boot) need liquid to move through. When depletion of the ground substance occurs, cell waste, inflammation, and important immune signals cannot get through, and they get stuck. Cellular waste can get trapped in an area that is drier than it should be, triggering inflammation. But then the inflammation that cannot get processed out of the area becomes chronic inflammation and chronic pain.

Perifascia surrounds *all* blood vessels. The actual vessel itself is fascia, and the blood vessels travel through your body to get blood to all your parts and to remove carbon dioxide and other waste. If your body becomes dehydrated and the fascia becomes thicker, blood cannot pass as easily, which you can imagine would create many problems. If you have a reduction in circulation to an area, you most likely have a fascia problem there. Fascia is also rich in nerve endings and sensory receptors. If the fascia gets dry and thick, there is potential for the nerves to get trapped in that thick fascia, which can develop into pain. There are so many reasons to keep your fascia healthy and hydrated, and this is actually a short list.

Keeping your body hydrated with enough ground substance keeps your immune system functioning properly. It keeps your muscles moving smoothly and your tendons and ligaments hydrated enough so they don't fray or tear. Hydration reduces compression on blood vessels and nerves. Maintaining your levels of ground substance allows the body to move cellular waste and process it, reducing chronic inflammation and allowing acute inflammation to do its job and get out of there. This is one reason why people who exercise tend to be healthier and have higher functioning immune systems. They've got healthy ground substance and their fascia isn't so stuck together, blocking the flow of immune cells and other important functions.

GOT INFLAMMATION? DON'T ICE!

Remember the old idea of RICE: Rest Ice Compression Elevation? Yeah. Don't do that. Even the doctor who first promoted that concept recanted it in 2015 because so many studies proved that RICE blocks healing, especially the rest and ice parts. Inflammation is an immune response. Swelling is a function of inflammation because your body is super hydrating the area to bring more immune cells, cells of repair, and the like to take care of itself. It's brilliant, actually. Remember that Jell-O sets when it gets still and cold? Rest and ice equals still and cold. They set and solidify your Jell-O, blocking your immune function, blocking your body's repair process. You want your Jell-O, your ground substance, your slickery matrix, to have lots of fluid and to be able to flow. Ice doesn't help you heal.

A couple of years ago, I ran excitedly out of my little cabin to paddle board with some friends. I had heard the waterfall we were to visit was a hundred feet tall and exquisite. I was so excited! Outside there was a light misty rain falling. I hurried out onto a little wooden staircase to load my car, except I slipped on the wet wood and severely twisted my ankle. I tore the flexor retinaculum, a band of fascia that keeps some tendons tacked down on the top of the foot. When it began to swell, and it got *huge*, it was the exact shape of that band of fascia. I was fascinated watching the whole process because *wow*! The *exact* shape of that retinaculum! I mostly stayed off my foot for a few weeks, but I never once iced it and didn't stop moving. I regularly pointed and flexed my foot, did little toe and ankle circles, did a bunch of non-weight-bearing movement to keep the tissue hydrated and guide the scar tissue as it formed. I released the trigger points, wanting to develop in my shins and calves. I put gentle weight on it for short periods of time. I healed pretty quickly considering the injury and now have full range of motion in that ankle and no recurring pain or dysfunction.

So how do we keep enough ground substance in the body? Can we just drink enough water to stay hydrated with slickery stuff? Do I have to eat Jell-O? The simple answer is no. To do that, you have to move. You have to move everything that you want to keep plumped up with ground substance, similar to only flossing the teeth you want to keep. Move it or lose it. Movement is one of the pillars of the FreeBody Method. How to move, and how often, is something we explore later in the book. For now, we need to lay the final bricks of the foundation by discussing the brain, stress, and pain.

PART 3

THE BRAIN, STRESS, AND TRAUMA

CHAPTER 11

The Brain and Stress

———

Have you ever noticed that your old back injury flares up when you're stressed? Do you get "tension headaches" when things feel overwhelming? It's quite common that the folks who seek my help actually began their pain journey during a major life transition, loss, or difficult event. Stress, and the stress response signaled by your brain, is actually a very big piece of the pain puzzle.

Over the next few chapters, I'm going to break down what a stress response actually is, what that means, and why it contributes to pain and inflammation. You'll learn why your old aches and pains tend to return when you get into stressful times, and I'll explain why stress activates back and neck pain specifically. I'm going to introduce you to your *Inner Neanderthal* and give you guidance on how to tame that inner cave person (we all have one!) so you can free yourself from the grip of chronic stress, tension, and pain.

CHAPTER 12

Stress, Trauma, and Pain

STUCK IN THE PAST

"Welcome to FreeBody," I said as Natalie walked in. She was in her mid-fifties and about as tall as I am, nearly five feet, ten inches. She had short, graying hair and a big smile. That smile held more urgency than warmth, more eager politeness than calm. She started talking about why she had come, right there in the waiting area in front of the door. Her voice was louder than it needed to be and came fast and furious. I encouraged her to hold on a moment, wait until I was ready to take notes, and to join me in my office where I could close the door and we could have some privacy. "Yes, yes, sorry, sorry. I'm just so excited to be here," she said. "I just know you're going to help me. I have *so* many trigger points."

As soon as I sat down and opened my laptop to take notes, Natalie started to yell-share her story. "I need your help! I've got trigger points all over my neck and I'm in a lot of pain!

My chest is full of trigger points and everywhere I touch it
just hurts and I don't know how to get rid of them and I tried
with a ball but that only hurt and I can barely move my neck
and now I'm getting headaches and my shoulders hurt and—"

"Pause a moment, please," I smiled at her. "Let's take a deep
breath together." She obliged. I watched her strain to take
that breath. It seemed everything was a strain, forced. She
was already so full of inhale that it was hard for her to take
more air in. She struggled to exhale.

When I began to work with her on the table, Natalie's body
was tense all over and she was unable to relax even a little
bit. Her breath was short and quick, her eyes were either
wide open or squeezed shut like she was trying to not see
something. I placed my hands gently on her chest and guided
her to breathe slowly. She couldn't do it. She couldn't breathe
slowly nor could she let go of her body and relax. Trying to
gently massage her felt more like wrestling. I felt that she
held something terrible, some horrible story inside her body.
Whenever I touched her, even barely touched her, she winced.
"There's a trigger point! And there's another one!" she said
to every single spot I laid my hands on. Her shoulders were
rounded off the table, her jaw clenched, and her muscles were
hard and unyielding.

I decided to just hold her head, breathe deeply myself, and
asked her how this all started. She blurted out that she had
been a victim of domestic violence and that her former boy-
friend had hurt her many times. I could see terror in her eyes.
She looked wildly around as if he could walk right in and
hurt her again at that moment.

I imagined that, considering the intensity of her current state, this must have happened recently. But no. Natalie explained that it had been over six years since the last incident. Six years. And she walked around scared to that day. I wasn't going to be able to get any trigger points to release, to coax her muscles to relax, until I could help her to breathe slowly and shift out of the stress response.

I started by gently placing my hands on her shoulders and pressed in just a little as I guided her breathing. I did not move my hands or look for trigger points. I just held them on her and told her body she was safe with me. I invited her to say internally, "I am safe. Right now I am safe," and to sigh audibly as she exhaled. I guided her to feel the table underneath her body. To feel the table holding her. "I am safe." After about an hour, she finally began to breathe more deeply and her muscles began to soften a little. The stiffness in her jaw slackened a bit. She started to feel safe enough to let go.

THREAT AND SAFETY

I want you to read that sentence again. "She started to feel safe enough to let go." That's really important because the brain prioritizes feeling safe at the cost of pretty much everything else. If you are in pain, cultivating a sense of safety within yourself becomes a priority if you want to escape that pain. In this section, I'm going to help you understand how stress is a lack of that sense of safety, and it contributes to your experience of pain. We will also talk about trauma, which is a kind of chronic stress. You'll understand more about how these contribute to how you feel in your body and ways to help yourself feel safer so you can feel your best.

To understand how trauma and stress affect the body and pain, we first need some understanding of the stress response and of trauma itself. The stress response is a biological reaction to something the brain perceives as a threat to the wellbeing of its human (Chu et al. 2022). This threat can be mental, emotional, or physical. It is something that threatens homeostasis, or everything working as it should. When the brain perceives a threat, it signals the stress response to begin. If the stress is overwhelming to the system, and the person gets stuck in the stress response, that is considered a traumatic event. The trauma is the response of the system, not the actual event itself. Something may be traumatizing to one individual and not to another. It depends on the brain and nervous system itself, and the meaning the system places on the event (Berkowitz 2023).

A trauma could be the death of a loved one. It could be a violent personal experience or a natural disaster. It could be a childhood. A trauma could be a narcissistic relationship or another type of an emotionally abusive relationship, something that shatters your self-esteem or your sense of safety. There's the lack of safety for people of color. There's the lack of safety of our LGBTQ+ community members. And that's trauma.

Trauma is lasting. It's sticky. It's not something the brain and body let go of easily. It begins with a stress response. The problem occurs when the person gets stuck in a stress response. This can become what is known as PTSD: Post

Traumatic Stress Disorder. It means that a person maintains a stress response long after the traumatic event because some part of them still doesn't feel safe. The brain has gotten locked in protection mode. And this is where chronic pain enters the picture.

When we are experiencing a stress response, many changes happen in the body. For our purposes we will focus on two important ways that stress and trauma effect our experience of pain. First, we will look at how the stress response activates tension in certain muscles. Then we will explore how the feeling of danger, or a lack of a sense of safety, increases our perception of pain. We will end this section with some ways to work with your brain to help you come out of the stress response to reduce your experience of pain and help you along your path of healing.

CHAPTER 13

The Stress Response

The number one job of the brain is to protect you, to keep you safe and alive. Inside your brain is the amygdala, a structure that is key to emotional processing, fear, and signaling other parts of the brain, namely the hippocampus, to activate the stress response. The amygdala is kind of the gatekeeper of your experience. It's the part that puts meaning to your experiences and decides if something is threatening or non-threatening. To do that, the amygdala is processing a bunch of sensory information. That sensory information comes in via the five senses and through **neuroception**.

Neuroception is a term coined by Dr. Stephen Porges, famous as the developer of the polyvagal theory. Neuroception means that our nervous system is a sense organ and it can detect danger, anxiety, or even calm (Porges 2009). Have you ever had the hair on the back of your neck stand up as you sensed there was some danger? Or have you ever had the experience when someone filled with anxiety walked into a room and, as you spoke with them, you felt anxious? Or have you ever known someone with a pleasant demeanor who always seemed calm and kind of happy, and you just felt good to be around them? That's neuroception. Your brain receives those internal signals and feeds the information for the amygdala to decipher.

The polyvagal theory states there are two branches of the **vagus nerve**, the nerve that swings us between emotional states, in and out of the stress response (Porges 2009). Briefly, the polyvagal theory says that we have three basic emotional states. The first is called our social engagement state, which is kind of our happy place. We enjoy others, we feel good, we are happy. According to polyvagal theory, this occurs when the ventral vagus nerve, or the front portion, is activated.

Next is the sympathetic activated state that can happen when a stressor, or threat, is perceived. This can become what is commonly known as the "fight or flight" response, or "mobilization." It is this response that we will focus on and call "sympathetic activation" and "stress response" interchangeably. The third state is freeze. In freeze, the nervous system has become overwhelmed by the stressor and the theory states that the dorsal vagus nerve, the back part, takes over and the person begins to shut down, goes into "freeze." This is termed "immobilization." They can't move, can't really think, can't speak well.

I witnessed this state very clearly when my daughter had a car accident. She turned left to get on the highway when another car crashed into the passenger side of her vehicle, totaling her car. A friend helped her get home and when I arrived, I found her on a blanket in the grass, staring out into space. She could barely utter any words and she moved very slowly, if at all. She was in freeze. I wrapped my arms around her and held her until she felt safe enough to cry and tremble, to work her way back into a sense of safety.

SYMPATHETIC ACTIVATION

Let's focus on the **sympathetic activation**, or fight or flight, state and how that influences our muscles. It's this sympathetic activation that seems to correlate more with pain and which I see most regularly in my practice.

Here's how the stress response happens in very simplified terms. When we experience something that the amygdala determines is a threat to our well-being, it sounds an alarm to other parts of the brain that there is a crisis and you are in danger. A signal is sent for epinephrine, commonly known as adrenaline, to be released. Epinephrine is what jacks things up. It increases your blood pressure to get more blood supply to your muscles so you have enough juice to punch or run your way to freedom. It opens the bronchioles in your lungs so you can get more oxygen to feed the muscles (Scott 2020).

Your sense organs are on hyper alert. For instance, your pupils dilate so you can take in more information through your sight, which means you might experience eye strain and light sensitivity with chronic stress. Sounds seem louder because your brain wants to be able to notice any sound that might alert danger, so it turns up the volume in your ears. This means that you might really hate the music that someone else is playing and not really be able to handle hearing it if you're in a stress response. The sensory receptors in your skin get amped up so you are more sensitive to things that touch your body, which means you might feel that annoying tag at the back of your shirt and it starts to drive you crazy.

Every time you drive a vehicle, your body goes into a little bit of a sympathetic activation so you are more alert and can catch dangerous situations on the road more quickly. This is why when you drive and look for an exit in an area you've never driven in, you might have to turn the music down to concentrate because suddenly the music sounds really loud. In someone who is highly stressed in general, that little sympathetic activation while driving is what turns into road rage. Someone who is already highly stressed cannot handle that extra epinephrine in their bodies and they go over the edge. You might perhaps notice that you tend to swear a lot more when you drive. Oh wait, that's me.

The sympathetic activation also increases contraction, or tension, in your muscles, specifically the flexor muscles of the body. The flexors are the muscles that curl things. The fingers might curl into fists. The legs get amped up to run. The hip flexors are the muscles that draw your knees toward your chest so you can run, or kick, or curl up into a ball to protect your vital organs, and they get stimulated to contract. All of these changes are biological and part of the autonomic, or automatic, nervous system. This all happens subconsciously. The amygdala receives information, it determines if there is a threat or not by assigning meaning to the information, and if it decides something is threatening, it will signal your systems into "fight or flight."

You might experience little activations, like what happens when you feel pretty good but you're driving. Those little activations can stack on top of each other, a little bit more epinephrine here and there, and the next thing you know you're "up to your eyeballs" in stress response. You might even say, "I just can't take any more today!" because the stress responses have stacked over the whole day, or weeks, or maybe longer. Learning to recognize when you are in a stress response and doing some self-regulation to bring yourself out of it can be a real game changer for people in pain, and frankly, for everyone.

A key factor in the stress response is the triggering of inflammation. I believe that your body is really pushing to get you to safety and you just might tear something in the process of fighting or fleeing. So our magnificent bodies trigger inflammation ahead of the injury to prepare to fix itself from the damage that may occur. That's my own interpretation and has no scientific basis, but it makes sense, right? Inflammation is a protector because it brings more fluid matrix, immune and repair cells to the area for healing. In a stress response your brain is trying to protect you. We'll talk more about inflammation and protection in the next chapter.

An interesting paper by Viktoriya Maydych linked the stress response, inflammation, and emotional attention. She found that the stress response triggers inflammation as well as negative attentional bias, or NAB (Maydych 2019). NAB means that we are looking for negativity, looking for things to be wrong when we are stressed. This is protective because we need to be able to notice when things are going wrong as they may pose a threat. This can be problematic in chronic stress because it can make us always looking for the bad in a situation, person, or relationship. Her paper relates it to depression. I would also add that it can keep us looking for pain and keep us finding it.

CHAPTER 14

The Amygdala and Danger in Me

THE AMYGDALA: OUR "INNER NEANDERTHAL"

The amygdala is a part of the limbic system in the brain. There are two amygdala, one on each side of the brain. These almond-shaped structures are part of the alarm system to keep us out of immediate danger. In early human times, the biggest danger was nature. Back then, you needed to run really fast and far, climb trees or mountains, or beat another human or animal to get to safety. The response of early humans to threats really needed to be strong to keep the humans alive. The flexor muscles needed a lot of power!

But now, our modern life itself is stressful but we still respond as if we're being chased by a tiger. There are bills to pay, and maybe your kid or loved one is suffering, or there are problems in your health, relationship, or job, and there are a lot of terrible drivers out there on the road to look out for! Modern life is *chronically stressful.* So there you are sitting at your computer or trying to talk to your angry teenager, your flexor muscles are all contracting strongly, and your heart is racing, but you have to stand there and keep doing what you're doing.

Tension builds up in the muscles, especially in the flexor muscles. Tension can lead to trigger points and trigger points can lead to pain. Travell and Simons indicate "emotional stress" as a cause of trigger points and include studies by psychiatrists treating their patients who have persistent pain (Travell, Simons, and Simons 1999).

I call the amygdala our *Inner Neanderthal* because it's in an older portion of the brain, developmentally speaking, and perhaps at this stage of human existence, a bit outdated in its responses. The amygdala determines whether or not we feel fear, among other things. It is taking in information and deciding whether or not it should trigger you into a sympathetic activation, to tell your body to get up and get going to safety. It's sort of like your inner cave person as its responses are not nuanced. If it senses something is dangerous, it grabs a club and starts smashing. This is helpful if you are being mugged, but not so helpful when you need to communicate with someone you care about during a rough patch in your relationship. Your Inner Neanderthal is the reason why you might overreact to something, might go into a strong sympathetic activation, a strong stress response, over something that isn't really life threatening at all. But it *feels* like a big deal. That's because if you're already in somewhat of a stress response and you get more stress activation, you might go overboard. Just like our road rage driver.

Think of it this way. You wake up to an alarm. That right there is, well, alarming. You get a little squirt of adrenaline and shoot up out of bed. Then you go to the kitchen to make coffee, but the coffee pot won't turn on. It's broken. Dang it! That's aggravating. And it's a little bit of a sympathetic activation in your system. Then maybe you get in the car to drive the kids to school after wrestling them into eating breakfast and gathering their things and, "Where is your other shoe!" and all that it takes to get kids out of the house. There's another little stress activation.

In the car, you get another little hit of adrenaline because you're on the road. When someone cuts you off to get into the school drop-off line, you find yourself swearing under your breath and dreaming of slashing their tires. As you sit in the unending line or traffic on the way to work, your hip flexors are probably really tense. You might start wiggling your legs or pushing your feet into the floorboards of the car. You might find yourself gripping the steering wheel as your knuckles turn white. Your back may begin to ache. All of this is a biological response that maybe is a bit overboard for the actual reality of things. But your Inner Neanderthal doesn't know that. It just knows that there are threats and sends signals. Your muscles contract and grip your bones, tension builds, trigger points are activated, and pain may make itself a home.

TRAUMA AND HYPERVIGILANCE

When a person experiences a traumatic event, the response of the nervous system might be to keep that person "on guard" because their nervous system experienced such a dramatic loss of safety. That Inner Neanderthal is going to go into overdrive, really looking for danger. When a person gets stuck "looking for danger," this is called **hypervigilance**. This can make things really tricky for that person because the amygdala might be sending them into a stress response during times of actual safety. But due to the trauma, they may not ever feel safe. Anxiety sets in. Muscles become tense. Inflammation and pain increase. Negative attentional bias becomes status quo and it's easy to be disgruntled, especially if you are feeling that old backache and can't move as freely as you did ten years ago.

I experienced PTSD and hypervigilance after a terrible ending to a challenging relationship. Every single car on the road that looked like his car sent me into a strong stress response. When I walked into work, I scanned the area to make sure he wasn't around. I lay in bed at night and trembled, which was actually a good thing! My body was shaking out the trauma and the stress chemistry.

I was nauseous and I struggled to eat enough, which led me to lose twenty pounds. I struggled to think clearly and couldn't focus because I was startled by any noise. I got stuck ruminating on those terrible experiences and feeling shame at having gotten myself into the situation and for letting it go on as long as I had. My back ached relentlessly, and I curled up in a ball in bed, trying fruitlessly to sleep. I just trembled.

Trembling is the body's way of getting that stuff out, of processing the stress chemistry, and reducing tension in the muscles that contract when in a stress response. In my Trauma Informed Yoga Therapy training, we learned about trembling as a way for the nervous system to release the burden of intense stress in the body. David Berceli, founder of TRE, Trauma Release Exercises, created an entire system of processing trauma by getting the body to tremble through specific exercises. Trembling or shaking can be helpful if you have experienced trauma or have PTSD. I recommend you look into TRE.

Natalie, the client I worked with who had been in a physically abusive relationship, was experiencing hypervigilance. She yelled when she spoke, couldn't breathe slowly and deeply, her eyes were wide open, and her muscles and jaw were clenched. She was "looking for danger" and her muscles had gotten so full of tension that everywhere hurt. I couldn't touch her body without her experiencing pain. She had learned that touch wasn't safe. She felt pain all the time.

Recall that I mentioned the fascia is full of sensory receptors. Studies are just beginning to shed light on how stress effects our fascial bodysuit. Yet I will say that my clients experiencing hypervigilance, like Natalie, feel thick and dense *all over*. Perhaps their fascia itself is "on guard." As research into the ways psychological stress effects fascia grows, I expect we will find that the fascia changes dramatically under the influence of stress and fear.

One of the things about hypervigilance is that our brain and body are responding to *imagined* danger. This is important because *what we think* actually strongly affects *how and what we feel.* This is an internal stressor on the system. If you've had a terrible experience, you might relate to ruminating, constantly thinking about the bad thing, and getting worked up over the memory as if it's happening right then and there. That's because the brain believes what it sees, even if what it sees is on a screen. That's why scary movies are scary!

Sometimes that screen is the movie playing in our minds. That internal movie affects our biological responses just as much as an actual event. It is real to the brain in that moment. This is the crux of trauma. When we get stuck thinking about it, worrying about it, picturing it, and fearing it, we send ourselves into protection mode and the stress response. If you are experiencing this, I'm going to teach you some ways to navigate yourself out of the stress response. I am here to let you know that you can, in fact, return to a sense of safety with some effort, understanding, and time. Time alone obviously doesn't work, as we see in Natalie's story. What we also learn from Natalie's story is that hypervigilance can lead to chronic pain.

I encourage you to work with a good therapist who understands trauma and the effects of trauma, perhaps a somatic therapist to help you process the physical repercussions of the trauma. Maybe you give TRE a try. When I was in PTSD, I knew that I needed to regain control of my nervous system, regulate out of the stress response, and stop feeding the stress response by getting out of hypervigilance. It was a journey, to say the least. But totally worth it. Freedom is exquisite. I did a lot of dancing and shaking.

DANGER IN ME AND PAIN

Professor Lorimer Moseley is a pain neuroscientist. He speaks of the "Protectometer" in your brain that determines how much pain you perceive in your body. Prof. Moseley describes the Protectometer as the part of your brain that determines how much protection your body needs around an area or tissue. That protection is experienced as inflammation and pain. When the brain has determined that something needs to be protected (remember that its number one job is to keep you alive and safe) it will send a signal of pain to limit what you're doing, thereby supposedly creating safety (Moseley 2019). Pain is protection.

His research has shown that there are two main factors in determining the response of the Protectometer, which means how much pain you will feel. Those factors are "Danger in Me" and "Safety in Me" or commonly shortened to DIMs and SIMs.

When the amygdala perceives something as a threat, that's a DIM. A DIM can be something like an actual injury, or it can be something emotional, like a worry or fear. DIMs can be unsupportive friends, a negative diagnosis, not understanding your diagnosis, a dysfunctional relationship, or an old trauma. A DIM could be losing your job or the loss of a loved one. All of those things, and more, can be experienced as a threat to your wellbeing. Studies show that the more DIMs we have, the more pain we feel (Moseley 2019). This is why so many of the people I work with that have recurring pain also have a story behind it. The more DIMs, the more pain you feel.

Hypervigilance is a DIM. It's a perception of threat and always looking for threat. That can keep you stuck in a pain cycle.

SAFETY IN ME

SIMs can be thoughts like, "My body is strong and I can heal." SIMs can be a supportive friendship or relationship, a kind neighbor, or understanding about your diagnosis. A SIM could be the knowledge that the disc degeneration on your MRI is actually normal wear and tear on the body and doesn't necessarily mean it's a problem or the actual cause of your pain. The studies tell us the more you can cultivate a sense of safety within, the less pain you will feel (Moseley 2019). I can attest to this in my own personal experiences and in my work with my clients.

Remember that when I worked with Natalie, I gently held my hands on her and had her repeat, "I am safe." I had her feel the table underneath her, bringing her more into the present moment and out of the fear from her past. This is what allowed her to cultivate that sense of safety. She literally spoke to her Inner Neanderthal and told her inner protector that she was safe. Her Inner Neanderthal started to get the message and began to allow her muscles to soften and her breath to deepen. You'll learn how to cultivate safety within yourself later in this section. You will also find videos of guided breathing and other self-regulation practices on the website, www.FreeBodyBook.com.

Earlier in 2022, I injured my back by doing a thing I always tell my clients not to do. I lifted a heavy table and as I twisted to put it down somewhere else, my back seized up pretty badly. Yikes! Terrible pain! I set the table down slowly and immediately got to the floor on my back with my knees bent and my feet on the floor. I took long, slow, deep belly breaths and told myself I was okay. I said, "I am safe. I'm going to heal. Everything will be fine." I didn't worry that I was fifty-two at the time nor thought that would impede my healing. I knew I would heal.

I tried dropping my knees side to side and when I went to the right just a couple of inches. *Ouch*! It hurt badly. I brought my knees back to center, took more deep breaths, and reminded myself that I simply pulled a muscle or some fascia but that my body is designed to heal. I did not for one second go into fear. I did smaller movements, breathed, and within a week, I was totally fine. I followed my own advice and did a lot of deep breathing, told myself I'd be okay, kept moving my body, watched my posture, and released my trigger points. That pain has not returned. No recurrence. No pain. No problem. Not giving in to fear is hugely helpful because you minimize the stress response to your injury, reducing inflammation and pain. Had I given in to fear, my body would have seized up even more, inflammation would have increased, and my pain would have been much worse. I may still be in that pain today. But I'm not.

CHAPTER 15

Stress and Your Back and Neck

———

Have you ever noticed that your pain is worse when you're stressed? Recall when I shared that during a period when I experienced PTSD, my back ached all the time. Stress activates certain muscles to contract, namely the flexor muscles, which can get them stuck in trigger points. Stress can directly lead to lower back pain and chronic neck issues. I'm going to break that down for you so you can understand why that is. If you are suffering from either chronic lower back pain, tension headaches, or other neck related issues, and you experience high stress and anxiety, this part is especially important for you.

THE PSOAS, STRESS, AND LOWER BACK PAIN

As I shared earlier when linking fascia to back pain, lower back pain is the leading cause of disability in 160 countries worldwide. Now I'd like to describe to you how stress signals certain muscles key to lower back pain to contract. That contraction can cause trigger points to activate and lead to pain directly along the lumbar spine. To do that I need to introduce you to your psoas muscle.

The deepest muscle in your belly is the **psoas**. The psoas muscle is the only muscle in the body that connects the upper body to the lower limbs. See the picture below. The psoas muscle runs along the front and sides of the lumbar spine. The upper attachment of the psoas passes through the back of the respiratory diaphragm at T12, the lowest of the thoracic vertebra (thoracic vertebrae have ribs attached to them) just above the lumbar spine. The psoas then runs downward along the sides of the discs and bodies of the lumbar vertebra, widening out like a sail as it descends, crosses over the pelvis at the groin, and joins with the iliacus muscle (which lines the inside of the pelvis) to attach below on the inside of the femur. The psoas pulls directly on the lumbar spine and discs.

The psoas, biomechanically speaking, is the largest of the hip flexor muscles, the muscles that draw your knees up toward your chest. This muscle will receive a strong message to contract when you go into a stress response. That psoas is going to try to protect you from danger by picking up your legs to run or kick. Have you ever had a really emotionally painful experience and it felt like you were kicked in the stomach? That's your psoas contracting and trying to get you out of there, and it's grabbing onto the spine in your lower back. I believe this is why so many people with anxiety and high stress have chronic lower back pain and dysfunction. I have seen this many times in my practice and felt it in my own body.

PSOAS

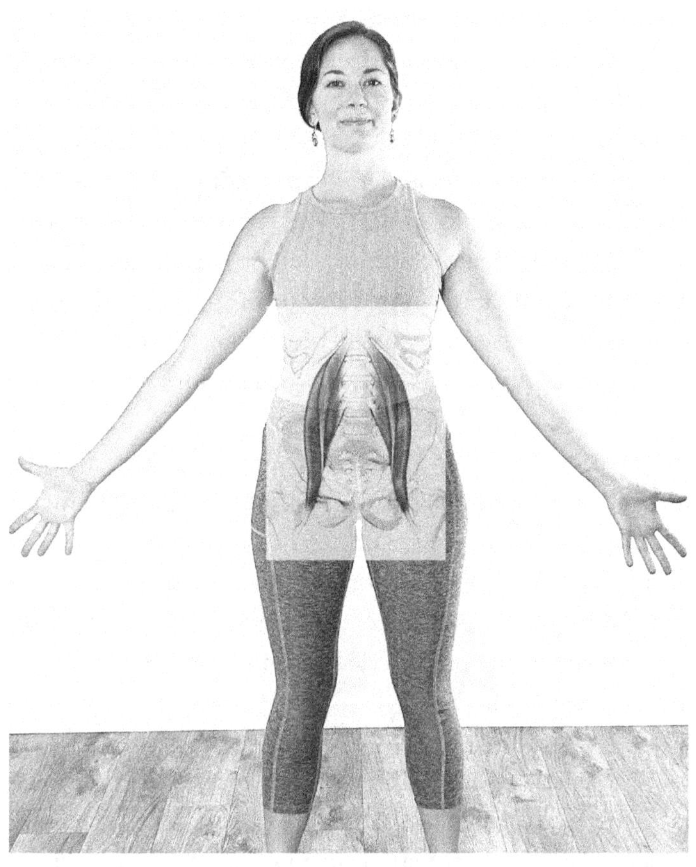

The psoas muscle. See how it grabs onto
either side of the spine?

Trigger points in the psoas muscle directly refer into the lower back along the lumbar spine (Travell and Simons 1993). Anyone who comes in to see me with an ache along their lumbar spine usually gets some relief from gentle psoas release work and lots of deep belly breathing. Deep belly breathing lowers the respiratory diaphragm as the belly pushes outward. When that happens, since the psoas muscle passes up and through the diaphragm, the diaphragm is literally massaging your psoas from the inside. It's kind of saying, "It's all right, dear. Everything's okay." That deep belly breathing is telling your Inner Neanderthal that you feel safe. It stops the flood of stress chemistry and can bring you out of a sympathetic activation. The psoas can then begin to soften and release its grip on your spine.

Interestingly, slow deep breathing has been proven to significantly decrease a person's experience of pain, reducing intensity and "pain unpleasantness" (Joseph et al. 2022). This means that slow deep breathing is already going to minimize pain. Adding the expansion of the belly to the deep breathing will also soften the psoas, release its pull on the lower back, and decrease back pain.

If we experience trauma and get stuck in the stress response, or if we just experience a lot of stress in general, the psoas muscle is going to get stuck in tension. A chronic stress response means the psoas will keep receiving a message to contract, to protect. Over time, that can lead to chronic lower back pain. I believe stress is a major factor in lower back pain that doesn't resolve within a month or so. I have seen that time and time again and lived it in my own experience. Part of that recurring pain is the fear about having back pain, fear that there is "something really wrong in there" because chronic pain is scary and worrisome. And then the fear of having the pain feeds the pain itself. Fear that "something is really wrong with me" is a DIM.

A word of caution: the psoas has a lot of delicate structures that lie over top of it, such as nerves, blood vessels, and intestines. If you are a massage therapist, you need to work very slowly and mindfully with the psoas, if you touch it at all. You can check out my second YouTube channel specifically for bodyworkers @FreeBodyMassage for clear instruction on psoas work. If you are not a bodyworker and working on your own psoas, I highly recommend you only use a soft air-filled ball to release it. Check out the website at www.FreeBodyBook.com for a video on how to release trigger points in your own psoas. You wouldn't want to compress your psoas with a lacrosse ball or other really firm object as you run the risk of compressing those delicate structures. Use a soft ball. Go slowly and sink in. Relax and breathe. You must approach the psoas with tender care. You cannot force the psoas into submission. It just doesn't work. It will protect itself by contracting.

STRESS AND THE NECK

When the stress response kicks in, the breath goes up higher into the chest and the breathing rate gets faster to send more oxygen to the muscles. This engages a set of muscles in the neck which lift the ribcage so you can get a bigger breath to run further or punch harder. Those muscles are called the **scalene muscles**. The scalene are two sets of muscles, one set of three muscles on each side of the cervical spine, the spine in your neck. They are the deepest of the neck muscles. When you are calm, the scalene do things like drop your head forward, rotate your cervical spine to turn your head, and tilt your head to the side, dropping your ear toward your shoulder.

The scalene are also cervical spine stabilizers, which means that when you fall or bump your head, they will instantly contract to protect that cervical spine. Anyone who has had a major accident such as whiplash or a big fall has had their scalene engage very strongly to protect their neck. There's most likely still trigger points in there if they've not been released.

A head injury like an accident or fall leads to a sudden contraction in the scalene muscles. Chronic stress leads to consistent contraction in the scalene muscles. When the scalene get stuck in trigger points, that tension can lead to a host of symptoms including compression of the discs in your neck. If one side contracts more strongly than the other, like the right side contracts more strongly than the left, the cervical spine gets pulled more strongly to the right. This pulling to the right side can lead to more pressure on the discs on the right, pushing them out to the left, leading to slipped or even herniated discs in the neck. This doesn't necessarily equate pain but it sure can cause problems.

NUMBNESS AND TINGLING

There is a nerve bundle called the brachial plexus that passes in between the anterior (or most toward the front) scalene and the middle scalene. When the anterior and middle scalene get "tight" or stuck, they can compress on that nerve bundle. The brachial plexus supplies nerves all the way down to your fingers. If you experience numbness, tingling, or radiating sensation or pain down to your fingers, the scalene are often the culprit. Check out the pain referral diagram for the scalene. You can see that it goes all the way down to the hand,

SCALENES PAIN REFERRAL

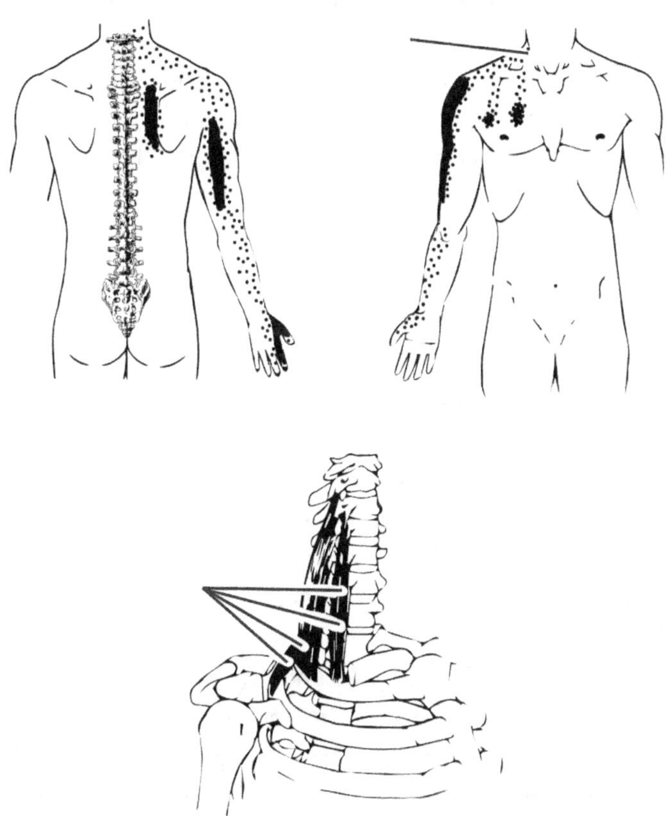

The pain referral patterns of the scalene muscles. See how trigger points in the scalenes can cause an ache in the chest, an ache numbness, or tingling down the shoulder, arm, and into the thumb and first two fingers?

perhaps to the thumb and first two fingers. Sometimes this is misdiagnosed as carpal tunnel syndrome.

Over time, scalene tension leads to a loss of range of motion in the neck. You might wake up and not be able to move your neck very much, and that might also include radiating numbness or pain down to the fingers. It will probably also include shoulder tension and crunchy shoulders. The neck and shoulders are directly related to each other. When the shoulders are tight, so is the neck, and vice versa. This tension can be released with that same air-filled ball you use on the psoas.

TENSION HEADACHES, DIZZINESS, AND TINNITUS

One other muscle to note that lifts the ribcage for stress breathing is the sterno-cleido-mastoid (SCM). The SCM attaches onto the clavicle (collarbone) and will lift the clavicle to pull the ribs up higher to allow bigger breaths. When you're calm, the SCM primarily rotates the head to the opposite side. But when you're stressed, it will lift the collarbone up so you can breathe more so you can fight or run from danger. If the SCM ends up holding on to that tension from contracting all the time in the stress response, you will have a harder time turning your head to one side. Interestingly, the SCM is also the number one muscle that causes headaches (Travell, Simons, and Simons 1999)! Those headaches can feel like sinus pressure, can wrap around your eye, will hurt on your forehead or back of the head, and can even cause dizziness and tinnitus, ringing in the ears. Hence, stress or "tension" headaches. If you have that annoying ringing in the ear, does it get worse when you're stressed?

SCM PAIN REFERRAL

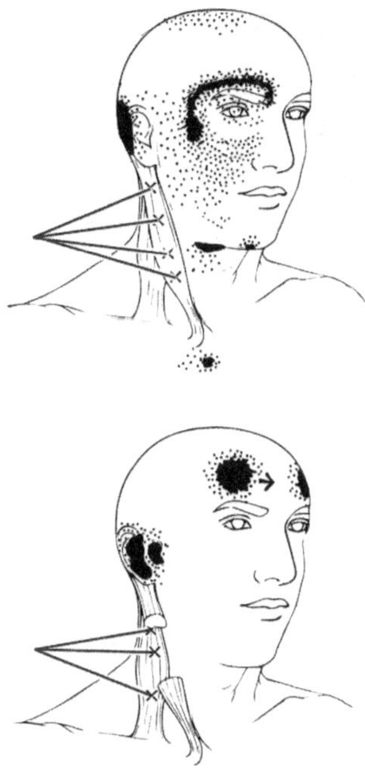

The sterno-cleido-mastoid, SCM, can cause a headache at the hack of the head, top of the head, or one that wraps around the eye, eye strain, sinus pressure, forehead pain, ringing in the ears, and vertigo-like symptoms.

You may have had a fall a few years ago that initially contracted your scalene and/or your SCM. Then the stress of life, or your fear around never recovering from that injury, might be the reason they got stuck in that contraction. "Getting stuck in that contraction" means there are still trigger points in those muscles.

Learning what happens in your own body when you go into a stress response is useful. When you can recognize that you're in that state in your mind and body then you can do something to change. You can choose a different state to be in. And once you get good at that, your trigger points and pain decrease. Let's go through some ways that you can recognize when you are in a stress response and ways that you can regulate yourself out of that so you can reduce tension, inflammation, and pain.

CHAPTER 16

Taming the Inner Neanderthal

———

HOW DO I KNOW IF I'M EXPERIENCING A STRESS RESPONSE?

As I mentioned, a stress response affects your breathing pattern, your muscles, your sensory organs, inflammation, and your heart rate. It actually affects much more than that, such as the immune system and digestion, but those are the things I focus on in this book as they are most relevant for this conversation. There are programmed ways that the human body noticeably responds when in a stress response that gives you clues that you're in stress. When you have these clues, you can stop what you're doing and regulate out of the stress response to reduce tension, pain, and inflammation. Why do I need clues? How come I can't tell if I'm experiencing a stress response?

The brain likes habits and can get stuck in the habit of activating the stress response. Many of us become habituated to being in stress and a sympathetic activation. We get used to being jumpy. We get used to pain and inflammation. We get used to anxiety. We get used to a negative attentional bias, so we tend to see the bad stuff, and that feeds our anxiety that we have gotten used to. After a while, we get so used to being in a stress activated state that we forget what calm feels like, what joy is. We feel stress, anxiety, and often, pain—the new normal.

To help you figure out what happens in your own body, I'm providing you with a list to check so you can see which of these things might happen inside you. Even though there are typical biological reactions to stress, each person does the stress response in their own way. This list in intended to help you become more aware of when you are in a stress response. Once you can notice when you are in a stress response, you can do something about it and soothe yourself out of that response.

COMMON PHYSICAL SIGNALS OF THE STRESS RESPONSE: CHECK THOSE THAT YOU RECOGNIZE IN YOURSELF

- holding the breath
- breathing up high in the chest
- short and rapid breathing
- eyes opened wide and pupils dilated
- eye sensitivity
- hands are in fists, jaw is clenched
- restless legs
- sweaty palms or feet
- sweating in general
- face has gone pale

- sounds seem loud and irritating
- tension anywhere in the body
- neck and shoulder pain
- back or hip pain
- headaches
- flare-up of any recurring pain
- peeing a lot

COMMON MENTAL AND EMOTIONAL SIGNALS OF THE STRESS RESPONSE:

- racing thoughts
- inability to focus attention on the task at hand
- confusion, can't make a decision
- can't speak thoughts clearly
- plotting revenge
- thinking about running away
- anger and frustration
- hatred and unforgiveness
- judging others/self-righteousness
- sadness
- feeling overwhelmed
- feeling excited
- ruminating (thinking about something incessantly)

SELF-REGULATION PRACTICES

Here is the light at the end of the tunnel! All of that talk about stress has perhaps made you feel a little stress response activated inside you, so let's learn some simple ways to help you regulate out of that. For many, the easiest hack is to change the breath. Breathing is something we can control.

As I said earlier, one thing that happens in a sympathetic activation is that your breath moves up and gets faster. Think about that for a minute. When you get scared, you gasp and breathe up in the chest. Your body is preparing to run or fight so it needs more air, more oxygen. You don't take a long, slow, deep breath and say, "Oh dear. I'm in danger." You breathe quickly, sharply, and high in the body and say, "Oh no!" That's stress breathing. And it's automatic.

Stress breathing is helpful when you're running scared, but not so good for the long haul. The simplest way to help ease your nervous system out of a stress response is belly breathing. Long slow belly breaths send a signal to your brain that you feel safe. I often add saying internally, "I am safe," just like I had Natalie do while I worked with her to ease her out of hypervigilance. I like to imagine I'm looking my inner cavewoman right in the eye, holding her hands, and telling her gently, "It's okay, honey. I am safe. We are safe. We can relax now."

Try it right now. Lie down on your back with your knees bent and your feet on the floor, a position which relaxes the psoas muscle. Take a couple of sighing breaths. Feel the back of your body on the floor. Feel the floor hold you up so you don't have to hold anything. You can relax and soften into the floor.

Rest your hands on your belly and press your belly into your hands as you breathe in. On the exhale, let your belly soften and drop without effort. Purposefully relax your muscles. On every exhale, let your body sink down a little more into the floor. Let your neck muscles relax. Let your shoulders soften. Are you clenching your butt? Let it go. Breathing in, the belly gently presses into your hands and your hands let your belly rise. Breathing out, relax your muscles more, sink into the floor a bit more. Soften. "I am safe. We are safe." Continue a few more breaths in this way, not worrying about counting your breaths or the length of them. Take moments throughout your day and pause, notice how you are breathing, if you are breathing at all.

I remember a story about my young friend, Candice, from a few years ago. I was with her and her brother one day when they were outside playing. Candice was ten and her brother was nine. I heard them yelling and ran outside to find them fighting and throwing things at each other.

Later on, once they had separated and taken some time to cool down, I spoke with them about the incident. I shared with them that our bodies give us signals to tell us when we are getting worked up in a stress response. When we learn those signals, we can pause, take some time out, and settle ourselves so we don't keep adding intensity, hopefully avoiding the yelling and throwing parts. I asked them if they could tell when they were getting angry with each other. Candice, who had been listening intently, opened her eyes widely and said, "Yes. I hold my breath! I notice that when I'm mad or upset I hold my breath." At ten years old, she could recognize that. Holding the breath means you are starving your brain of oxygen and that is definitely going to get that Inner Neanderthal up in arms to try to save you by increasing the intensity of your stress response.

Candice made a plan that when she was getting upset at her brother, she would check her breathing and see if she was holding her breath. If she was, she'd take a break and go do some deep breathing instead of continuing to feed that stress response, letting things escalate. If a ten-year-old can do that, so can you. I believe in you.

Develop the habit of checking your breathing every couple of hours throughout the day. Set a timer on your phone that reminds you to check your breathing and to pause a moment to take a few long, slow belly breaths. Then you can get back to things with more ease in your body, and your brain. In this way, you will soothe your brain out of a stress response regularly instead of letting it stack throughout your day. This powerful but simple practice can transform your experience, and your experience of pain. Remember that turning off the sympathetic activation stops the flow of the chemicals that lead to chronic muscle tension, inflammation, and pain. And long, slow, deep breathing directly decreases pain intensity.

SHAKING OUT THE STRESS CHEMISTRY AND REDUCING PAIN

One absolutely fabulous way to regulate your nervous system out of stress is to shake your body all over. I've worked with anxious folks who shared that focusing on their breath made them more anxious. They couldn't do it. So if that's you, instead of focusing on the breath try moving instead. There's a reason for that saying, "Shake it off." It works!

Since stress chemistry activates tension in your muscles, it can be very helpful indeed to spend some time shaking out your body. Here's a way to do that:

1. Stand in the middle of the room so you don't hit anything. Make sure there's space around you.
2. Begin by shaking out your arms. Wave them all over the place, shaking them high overhead, shaking out to the sides, letting your hands remain loose and flappy.
3. Then stand on one leg and shake your other leg out for about twenty seconds. Then switch legs. You can hold on to a chair or countertop if you need support to keep your balance.
4. Let it fly! Shake it all loose and shake it out.

Alternatively, you can put on your favorite dance music and have a little dance party with yourself for a few minutes. This is my favorite way to get that chemistry and tension moved out of my muscles and body. Dance! Have fun! Fun and enjoyment is an excellent way to shift out of the sympathetic activation and get yourself back into the ventral vagus, or your happy place. Remember to check the book website at www.FreeBodyBook.com as I've included a guided shaking practice to support you.

Here's a story to tie this all together. I was house sitting for some friends one time and went out early in the morning to get some fresh air and take in the mountain view. Their door is funny in that if it's unlocked from the inside it can still be locked on the outside. It's a fire safety thing.

I went outside in my socks on a cold January morning. The world was quiet and peaceful around me, and when I tried to get back inside, I learned that I was locked out. I didn't have my phone and all the other doors were locked. Oh no! My breath immediately got short and sharp, my eyes opened wide, and I searched quickly around to see if there was some other way to get in. I thought, *"Well this is interesting. I'm about to watch my stress response kick in!"* And sure enough, it already had. My heart and thoughts both started racing. *"What will I do? They're out of the country and I need to be teaching online from my clinic in three hours!"*

I began to sweat, even though I was cold. I could feel my heart pounding. I felt "something" in my lower back, though not quite pain yet. I heard some ringing in my ears and felt a strong urge to pee. I remembered we have a mutual friend a couple of miles away, so I literally began to run down the mountain to get to her, and her phone, to ask them to remotely unlock the door from an app, which they did. The running actually felt really good, except for the part that I had no shoes and it was January in the mountains. My body was happy to run because it wanted to get away from this danger.

Once I arrived at my friend's house and she opened the door, I burst into tears. I said, "Don't worry. I'm actually fine. It's just the stress chemistry!" We got me inside the house and I later logged on to teach with ten minutes to spare. I am actually somewhat glad it happened as it was really cool to observe my system in action.

Your brain is ultimately just trying to keep you alive. Your Inner Neanderthal is going to react when it feels a threat and activate a stress response. We can get stuck in that sense of threat, or Danger In Me, with trauma or hypervigilance, which can lead to persistent pain.

To notice when you are in a stress response and regulate out of that using your breath and movement, like shaking, can significantly reduce your experience of pain. Over time, your Inner Neanderthal becomes less reactive as you spend less time in that stress chemistry. You feel better overall.

Now we have a fuller picture of pain in our bodies. Trigger points are tension in our muscles which cause limitation, inflammation, and pain. Fascia is the site of inflammation and sticky dehydrated fascia is a key player in the pain we feel. When the brain detects a threat or stress, the Inner Neanderthal signals a stress response, which increases tension and inflammation. These three together must be addressed to heal pain and get back to living. We will now begin to look at how to take care of our bodies to reduce and avoid pain. Our first step is to explore posture and discover that how you sit and stand makes a huge difference in how you feel.

PART 4

POSTURE

CHAPTER 17

Why Good Posture Matters

THE IMPORTANCE OF POSTURE IN AVOIDING PAIN

Your posture can either support you or cause you suffering. The definition of posture is the position you take when you sit or stand. So the position you *regularly* take when you sit or stand becomes your postural home. Position becomes posture. Because our brains like habits, your posture becomes a deeply ingrained habit. Unfortunately, we often get stuck in a posture that misaligns our bones and creates imbalanced tension in our muscles and fascia, pulling some muscles chronically long and putting others chronically short. Neither side of that equation is going to be happy in the long term because muscles don't seem to like being chronically short or long. Muscles that are chronically short or long develop trigger points and that leads to pain.

Fascia responds to the demands you put on your body. How you sit and how you stand sends signals to the fascia to get thin here and thick over there. It molds and shapes itself depending on your posture. Fascia can turn itself into thick straps when you hang yourself on your bones instead of using your muscles as they are designed, that is to keep you upright and in a more neutral position.

When you have pain, if you keep getting stuck in the same old posture, you may be feeding the tensional system that causes your pain. When I had sciatica, my right hip was high. I kept finding myself standing with my weight over to the right. Standing over my right leg kept feeding the trigger points in my low back, hips, and inner thighs that had led to my sciatica symptoms. Some muscles overworked while some were underused. Both overworking and underworking muscles develop trigger points. They ache.

Let's talk about how posture trains your body, why it can be so hard to change it, and key ways that certain postures lead to pain and suffering. Then I'll share with you some information on what good posture looks and feels like so you can go about the business of mindfully shifting to better posture, and a happier body. Good posture is one of the Five Points of Freedom in the FreeBody Method.

CHAPTER 18

Your Postural Home

Our bodies are designed on a skeletal template. While every person's skeleton is unique, there is a basic template to the human skeleton. The bones are designed to be in an optimal position relative to each other. When we stray away from that optimal position, such as slouching or constantly standing with the weight over one leg, we set up a host of issues in the tissues. We train our bodies that the non-optimal position is our "postural home." The muscles and fascia adjust to this "home" and some muscles will get weak over time.

For instance, if you slouch a lot, your back muscles get pulled long and long muscles tend to get weak over time and their fascial bags get thin and prone to injury. When you try to sit up well, the middle of your back might ache, perhaps from the erector muscles (the muscles along your spine that lift the spine erect) working so dang hard to hold you up. You may have noticed that. I recently worked with a thirteen-year-old boy who came in with a backache that wouldn't go away. He said he kept trying to sit up but his back ached relentlessly every time, right across the middle, below his shoulder blades.

That is a typical response as the muscles regain strength and the fascia changes. But that goes away so don't give up!

Since our brains like habits, that postural home, even if it's causing some aches and pains, begins to feel normal and sitting up well starts to feel not normal. Your postural home is comfortable in a way, even when causing pain, because you may not identify it as a source of your pain. To change it can feel weird. That is partly because of **proprioception** and partly because of **muscle memory**.

PROPRIOCEPTION

Proprioception is how your body knows where it is in space. You can reach your arm back behind you so you cannot see it, but you still know where your arm is. There are sensory receptors throughout the fascia in your entire body that feed information to your brain about where things are, how much contraction there is in the muscles, the distortion of the fascia, the angle and pull on your joints, and the pull on the tendons. All that information tells your brain where your body parts are. Proprioception gives feedback about the state and location of your joints and tissues. I believe it also contributes to how our muscles are used and which ones are going to get used and in what order. That's called the **muscle firing pattern**. There is no clear scientific understanding of how the muscle firing pattern is determined and signaled by the brain. Frankly, we can't yet explain a *lot* about our bodies. This body is a miraculous wonder! We've much to learn. Yet I believe that our proprioception has a lot to do with it because where we are in space and where we want to go are intimately connected. Getting to point B requires a certain muscle firing pattern to get there.

Here's an example of how proprioception affects the muscle firing pattern. Have you ever had to walk down a flight of stairs in the dark? When you got to what you thought was the bottom stair, you thought that you were stepping out onto a floor, but there was actually one more stair to step down. That step down felt like a bottomless hole that you were falling into. That's because your muscles were set for you to step forward but you, in fact, had to step down. That second or two when your body had to reorient itself is directly related to where your body thought it was in space and where it thought it was going. Based on your body's awareness of where it was in space, your proprioception, it determined which muscles were going to contract and in which order so that you could safely step forward. Except you had to step down, which changed the whole contraction pattern entirely. A totally different muscle firing pattern was needed. So it feels like you're kind of lost in space as your brain figures out that you're not actually going where you thought you were going, and changes the muscle firing pattern. Now how does this relate to posture?

Your proprioceptors are telling your body where it is at all times. And given that the brain loves habits, it becomes acclimated to a particular posture and the muscles engage in a certain way to hold you in that posture. Again, over time that becomes your postural home which means that it's going to feel the most normal for you to be in that particular position. Your proprioceptors become acclimated to that posture and when you're in that posture, they're kind of sending a signal to tell your brain, "All good here. We're home." Proprioception, then, may program the muscles in a way that keeps you landing home. And that home is often feeding tension, fascial imbalance, and contributing to pain.

MUSCLE MEMORY

We tend to think about muscle memory when we are building muscle strength and training in music, dance, or sport. It's commonly known that when you build muscle, the muscle "remembers" how to be strong or how to do particular movements so you eventually can do them without thinking. If a pianist had to think about how to move their fingers over the keys every time they played, they'd never improve. They play scales, chords, and a piece of music over and over to train that memory into their tissues so they won't have to think about it when they play. Same with a dancer. My daughter is a professional ballerina. I have seen her practice the same twirls and jumps for many years to keep up her skill. Her muscles remember how to do each movement so her dancing looks effortless, even though it has taken her years of effort to get there. That's the idea, right? Her body responds to that lifelong training by remembering her position, which muscles to engage, how much to engage them, and which muscles to relax at certain times so that she dances like a river flows, smooth and fluid.

When you are in a position for a long time and it becomes a posture, that partly means that your muscles have built memory of that position. Certain muscles will engage and certain ones will relax. Over time, that posture becomes embedded into your muscle memory so you don't have to think about it. It's just what you do. You might always sit on the right side of the couch because it's just where you always sit. When you are there, you might always tuck your right leg under you or lean off to the right to rest on the arm of the couch. Over time, it feels weird to sit another way. Again, some of your muscles will, over time, become weak from underuse and they might ache. Their fascial bags grow thin and the risk of injury increases.

Do you always sit on one side of the couch or sleep on the same side of the bed? Do you always sleep on your side and on the same side of your body every night? Are you starting to wonder if that's a good idea? Try changing it up, move to the other side of the couch, or sleep on the other side of your body to interrupt the old pattern.

When I spoke with Amber Davies, the trigger point therapist who co-authored *The Trigger Point Therapy Workbook*, she shared about things that keep trigger points coming back and can keep you in nagging aches and pains. When we discussed why posture is a driving force for the development of trigger points, she said, "Muscles learn." That means the same muscles, and the same parts of the muscles, will contract time after time. Since the body responds to the demands you put on it, it will learn a dysfunctional pattern if that is what you tell it to do.

Amber described a scenario of a woman sitting on the couch and her partner always sitting on her left side. The woman sits with her laptop on her lap and her partner to the left. If the couple always sits in this way, the woman is going to turn her head to the left all the time to chat with her partner every night as they watch TV. That will most likely cause her some issues in her neck. The laptop in her lap may strain her shoulders and the woman will always be looking down, further straining the neck, not to mention some strain in her back. Amber pointed out that "those habits, those little, tiny habitual things that we're doing, add up." Habitually sitting on the same side of the couch or your person gets ingrained into the tissues and might be an underlying cause, a perpetuating factor in your pain. Amber said, "Maybe you switch places, prop the elbows up, get up and get some movement, do some self-trigger-point release." Basically, you've got to change your habits. It's not easy at first, but it's worth the little bit of effort it takes. I'll show you how to get into good posture later in this book. Videos are also available on www.FreeBodyBook.com.

WHY CHANGING YOUR POSTURE FEELS WEIRD

When you attempt to change your habitual posture, you will notice that it's pretty challenging at first and it's not just the muscles being weak. It just feels weird to be in a different position because of proprioception. If you've ever tried to stop chronically crossing your legs, you will notice that it feels really strange to sit without your legs crossed. I think it took me years to stop doing that all the time, even with dedicated effort. It also took me a long time to stop habitually standing on my right leg, with my hips shifted over to the right. When I stood on both feet, it just felt off and it was a little irritating. I felt muscles that I wasn't used to feeling when I was standing centered. That's because the muscles that I used to stand on both feet were different than the muscles I used to stand with my weight over to the right. From a fascia perspective, my fascia bodysuit had molded to the shape of standing off to the right and kept pulling me over there.

As things shifted to center, it took some time for my brain and body to get acclimated to the new position. My muscles were used to holding a particular pattern of engagement to keep me in my postural home. My proprioception and muscle memory had trained to that position, even though it was contributing to my pain. When I started to change it, muscles that had been kind of asleep had to engage in a whole new way and they tired more easily at first. My fascia bodysuit needed time to reshape itself so I was centered and not off to the right. I regularly found myself back in my old poor postures. If you've ever tried to change your posture, you know what I'm talking about.

Don't beat yourself up if you're attempting to change your posture and finding it difficult. You are not only having to build strength in certain muscles but you also have to get over the strange feeling of being in a different position. That takes time to re-program into your body and brain. It can be quite irritating to your systems for you to put yourself in a different position. It's worth the effort if you're dealing with pain or dysfunction because your posture is, often, a part of your recurring pain problem. Standing on my right leg all the time was directly feeding my sciatica symptoms and changing my posture was a key element of my healing. I'm going to share more about posture, sciatica, and hip issues in just a little bit.

If you're reading this because you're experiencing pain in your body, check your posture. How do you sit? How do you stand? Do you slouch and round your shoulders and hang your head forward? Do you always sit off to one side? Do you always stand with your weight on one leg? Are you always crossing your legs, and the same leg over the other? The first step in changing anything in your brain and body is awareness. You first become aware of how you are doing things and how often. Then you can begin to take the steps to make positive changes.

Let's look at some common postures that can lead to pain over time. I want you to understand why these are not helping you so you can start to make changes to support your healing.

Posture and Neck Pain

Luke is a tall, kind gentleman. He's the sort of man you just feel safe with, like he'd bring you tea and cookies and tell you how much he loved his dog when he was a young boy.

Luke came to me after retiring from a decades-long career as a veterinarian, caring for animals his whole life. He performed a lot of surgeries and spent his adult life either leaning over an operating table or crouching down to attend to someone's beloved pet. I imagined him earnestly performing his surgeries, getting closer to take great care. And this eventually caused him to have pretty severe and chronic neck pain.

Being tall, Luke was always going to lean forward a bit to meet the rest of us. By the time he came to see me, his head was craned permanently forward of his shoulders and his chest was drawing in. These are the classic signs of someone who has curled inward most of their lives to look down. Many of my clients that suffer with sadness have this posture. And many of the tall clients do too.

I recall a client named Theresa who came to me in her sixties. She was strong and commanding at almost six feet tall. She came to see me because she had chronic tension headaches and neck pain. Nothing had helped her with her pain for more than a few days. She shared that her husband was a military officer who stood several inches shorter than Theresa. She often shrank herself to allow him to be as big as possible. (My words, not hers.) I could see it when they stood together. She rounded her shoulders forward and dropped her head as soon as he was near her, making herself smaller. Theresa felt great relief in just the first session of trigger point therapy and was excited to release her points herself at home. But if she kept rounding to get smaller, her pain and those trigger points would always return. Understanding that her posture was contributing to her headaches and neck pain, she was committed to stand tall, open her chest, and lift her head. I stayed in touch with her for over a year and she was able to remain pain free with a little effort.

But Luke was different. He had at least another decade on Theresa and his work had required him to look down and lean forward all day for many years. He didn't take a lot of breaks from that position, much like people who look down at their laptop and phone all day. Sound familiar? The problem is that eventually his bones stuck that way and his discs had deteriorated from the misalignment of his spine. His fascia became hard and thick. His poor neck and shoulder muscles felt like rocks, hard and unforgiving. They had spent decades trying to pull his head back over top of his shoulders instead of letting it hang forward, out of optimal position.

If he had taken breaks and opened his chest and looked up, released some of those trigger points along the way, moved and freed his fascia, his body would be very different right now. But instead he spent most of his time hanging his head forward, and the muscles kept working hard to pull it back up.

There is a muscle called **levator scapulae** whose job is this very thing. Levator scap begins on the inner upper corner of the shoulder blade (scapula) then rises up and attaches along the sides of the vertebra in the neck. It lifts your shoulders up toward your ears, elevating the scapulae, but it also pulls your head back when you are in what's called "forward head posture." It means just what it sounds like. Your head is dropped forward. This is the position you are in when you look down to text, look down at your computer for work, or look down for anything. Then those levator scapulae muscles, and the muscles on the back of your neck, get pulled long and they contract really strongly to lift your head back up. If you don't actually lift your head, that contraction gets stuck as trigger points. This is what was going on with Luke. And it had been going on for a very long time.

I could help him a little bit, but not as much as I'd have liked, because his body had gotten so tight and compressed and now, after many years, his spine had literally changed its shape. Due to the deterioration of his discs from all that compression, his neck wouldn't be able to go back to its intended position, returning his head over his shoulders. His spine had shifted from its original design. This means his muscles will always be in a compromised position and the fascia will always be dehydrated due to limitations in his movement. Those neck and shoulder muscles will most likely carry a lot of trigger points amidst the other problems that chronic forward head posture can cause. He can release those trigger points regularly and find some ease, which he does, but he will struggle with the effects of that posture from now on. Don't let this happen to you! Stop looking down all the time. Really. Take breaks to look up regularly throughout your day. Hold your phone up instead of down by your belly.

Luke's fascia had hardened to help hold his head. Tom Myers speaks of this in his book, *Anatomy Trains*. He explains that in forward head posture, the fascia around the muscles that are "locked long" to hold the head will thicken into straps and become dry and very sticky (Myers 2001, 18).

Luke is an excellent example of how important your postural habits are for the long-term health and ease of your body. The human body is a template while each individual body is its own unique expression of that template. We are basically all designed, barring genetic abnormalities, to have bones that are arranged a certain way and in a certain relationship to each other. The cervical spine, the neck, arises out of the thoracic spine, where the ribs are, and has a little bit of a curve forward and then holds the head centered over the shoulders. That's the optimal position.

Every muscle in the body is designed to attach to, and pull on, the bones in a way that maximizes their effectiveness, called leverage. When we move our bones out of their optimal position, we affect the leverage of the muscles. The muscles don't like that and they will contract to try to bring you back to that optimal position. This leads to trigger points, thick fascia, and in this case, neck and shoulder pain and headaches.

Of course our bodies are designed to move and not be stuck in one position, even the optimal one. Of course! Yes, move and move some more! Hanging your head to cry because you are sad isn't going to give you chronic headaches. But hanging your head all day long to work or scroll on social media just might create the tension in your muscles that leads to chronic neck pain and headaches. That position shifts the orientation of the bones from optimal, taxes the muscles by taking away their leverage, and thickens the fascia. Let's look more closely at this forward head posture and learn why getting stuck in forward head posture is so problematic.

FORWARD HEAD POSTURE

The classic way to describe the effects of forward head posture is to compare the weight of your head to a bowling ball. For easy math, let's say that's ten pounds. Your neck and shoulder muscles are designed to hold that ten-pound bowling-ball-head over your shoulders while maintaining a little curve in your cervical spine. Yes, you are designed to be able to move your head, look around, look down, look up, tilt your head and more. Yet, the design is optimized when the head rests with the ears basically centered over the shoulders, so you can look and move forward. See the picture below of my friend, Alice. Check out how her ears are over her shoulders which are over her hips and her ankles. That's great posture!

GOOD POSTURE

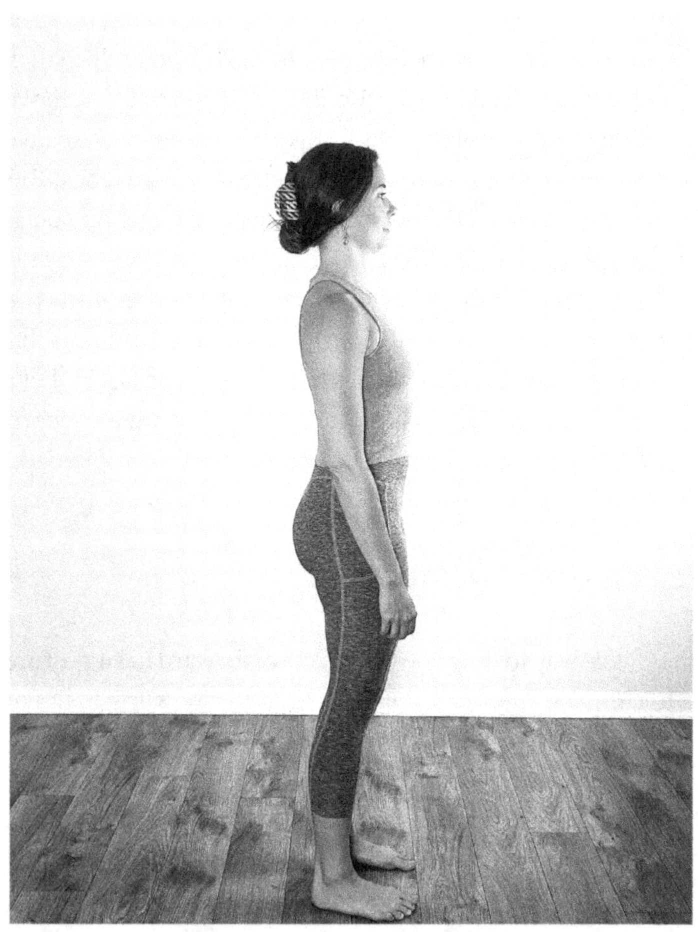

Good posture. Ears over shoulders over
hips over ankles.

For every inch your ears move in front of that shoulder line, you add the weight of another bowling-ball-head to the muscles which are not designed to hold your head out there for long periods of time. This means that when you hang your head down to text on your phone and your ears land four inches in front of your shoulders, about a forty-five-degree angle, your neck and shoulder muscles are now holding up five bowling-ball-heads instead of just one. Fifty pounds instead of ten (Aliberti et al. 2020). You can imagine holding a bowling ball in your hands close in to your body, and then holding it in front of you with your arms outstretched. Your arms will get tired *way* faster holding that bowling ball out in front of you, and the same thing is happening in your neck every time you text or look down at your computer. This leads to chronic neck and shoulder pain and tension (Aliberti et al. 2020). It also turns the fascia around those neck and shoulder muscles into hard straps.

Once in a while that's okay. But if you habitually look down at your phone or laptop, or at an operating table to perform surgery on little cats all day like Luke, your neck and shoulder muscles get real tired. And angry. They'll end up holding a lot of trigger points, and that can cause you pain, headaches, neck pain, and even eye strain. This was proven in 2020 by a study of people who used a smart phone all day long. Many had chronic neck pain (Aliberti et al. 2020).

The fascia turns into straps to help the poor and weakened muscles (remember trigger points make muscles weak, besides the loss in leverage.) That fascia gets thick and may become burdened with inflammation. Leather-like strap is not the ideal state for fascia. Remember that once fascia is thick and stuck, inflammation cannot move out of it, blood supply diminishes, and nerve impingement may occur.

LOOKING DOWN AT PHONE

Looking down at the phone AKA "text neck" posture.

Now imagine looking up, as in the next picture. Once your head is moved in front of the shoulders and you look forward to perhaps walk around, the muscles near the base of the skull get squashed while they hold the full weight of five

FORWARD HEAD POSTURE

Notice the rounded shoulders, ears are forward
of the shoulders.

bowling balls. The upper part of the trapezius works real hard, along with some little muscles called the suboccipitals. Tension in those muscle groups can lead to chronic headaches, which I have seen thousands of times with folks who have forward head posture.

NECK AND SHOULDERS TOGETHER

The connection of the shoulders to the neck is important to understand. I've never seen anyone with forward head posture that didn't also have shoulders that were rounded forward and curled inward like Luke's. The neck and shoulders work together. When the shoulders round forward and you slouch, the head drops forward and the neck muscles get strained. Try it right now. Sit up for a moment with your head held high and look forward. Now let yourself collapse forward, rounding the shoulders and notice what happens with the head. It moves forward, yes? Notice how your neck feels. Now try turning your head side to side while you stay slouched forward. Hurts right? Yeah. That doesn't feel good.

Now try leaving your shoulders rounded forward and pulling your head back over your ears. That feels terrible! It doesn't work because you cannot leave the shoulders curled inward and pull the head back. If you have tried to get your head back over your shoulders without attention to the collapse of the chest, this is why that didn't work. Open your chest first, then lift the head.

The stage has now been set for some pretty awful neck pain, besides the headaches and all the other things I mentioned above. One of the overworked muscles in forward head posture is the trapezius. We met trapezius in the trigger point section. The trapezius attaches at the base of the skull, so forward head posture hangs those five bowling balls on the trapezius. The trapezius also attaches along the top ridges of the shoulder blades. Rounding the shoulders draws the shoulder blades forward and pulls on the trapezius in that way. Forward head posture pulls the trapezius in multiple directions, and it gets pretty unhappy about it.

Check out that trapezius pain referral picture again. It includes: neck pain along the side of your neck, a headache that wraps around the side of the head to the temple, aching in the eye, a nagging ache in the jaw. Trapezius headaches can include nausea and aching at the base of the skull. Does any of that sound familiar to you? Have you been diagnosed with migraines because you get nauseous headaches that throb in your temple and cause eye strain? Check your posture, open your chest, and release your trapezius.

TRAPEZIUS PAIN REFERRAL PATTERN

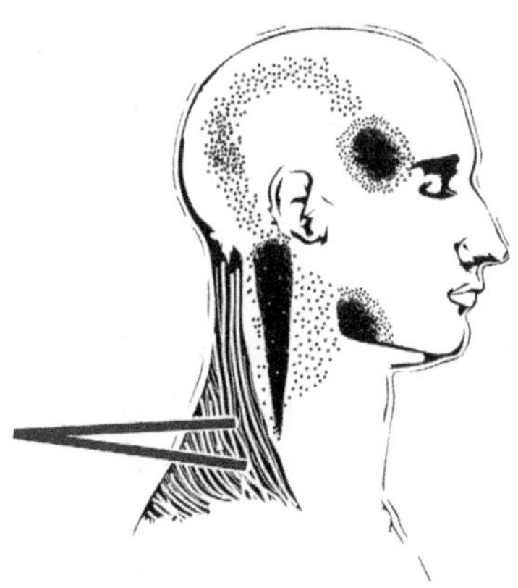

Common pain referral pattern of the upper trapezius. The lines point to where the trigger points tend to develop. The shading indicates where people who have those trigger points report that they feel pain or sensation; neck and jaw pain, pain at the temple, a headache that wraps around the side of the head, pain behind the eye, nauseous headache.

BACK TO LEVATOR SCAPULA

Again, one of the jobs of levator scapulae is to *resist forward head posture* and pull your head back over your shoulders, back to that optimal position. When you hang your head forward, the levator scap is grabbing the sides of your neck along its upper attachments, trying desperately to get your head back over your body. My experience is that, even though the textbook pain referral pattern is a deep ache at the intersection of the neck and shoulder, it can also create pain along the sides of the neck where those attachments are hanging on for dear life. I always release trapezius and levator scap in the same session.

A friend mentioned to me that her mom was having bad pain on the side of her neck after years of leaning over a desk for work, writing and typing much of the day. She'd had the pain for years but now that she was retired, she was finally ready to deal with it. Her neck aches all the time. She has terrible headaches, difficulty turning her head side to side, and has trouble sleeping because she can't get comfortable. Her head and neck constantly ache. Later I found out that her mom's pain had gotten so bad that she couldn't get any relief until she got botox shots in her levator scapula. She went to see a doctor to get poison injected into her body to literally paralyze the muscle that was causing her neck pain. Botox will work for a short period of time and it won't do anything for her headaches or the inability to turn her head and many of her other symptoms, but it did help with the neck pain. She will need to keep having that poison injected into her body because she doesn't know how to release her own trigger points and doesn't want to learn. Unfortunately, at this point, her spine may have shifted so much, like our friend Luke the vet, that she will always experience some issues. Not to mention those hard fascial straps.

I'm telling you: stop looking down all the time! I've seen it before and I'll see it again and I bet someone reading this is having that neck pain right now. Don't forget that often tension in the shoulders can cause that pain along the side of your neck, and please don't wait until you retire to do something about it. I'd rather your story end like the Theresa, who, even in her sixties, was able to get pain free after many years of headaches and neck pain. You really can get yourself free. Even Luke experiences far less pain than he used to. It's never too late to get some relief, if not total freedom, from pain.

Here are some simple things related to posture and your neck that you can do to help yourself to keep your neck happy, even if you have to work on a computer all day.

- Set your laptop up on a box and use a wireless keyboard so you can look forward, even slightly up perhaps, when working on your computer.
- Regularly take breaks to open your chest and look up, squeezing your shoulders blades together as you do.
- Practice holding your phone up higher when you scroll and text instead of holding it close to your belly and looking down.
- When you stand, stand tall. Own your whole self!

Now that your neck is going to feel better, let's look at postures that relate to sciatica and hip pain.

CHAPTER 20

The Postures of Sciatica and Hip Pain

Got sciatica and can't seem to get rid of it? Does your hip (or butt) ache and you can't sleep on it, so you flip from side to side and still can't get comfortable? Do you want to avoid these problems? If you answered yes to any of these questions, this chapter is very important to you. In fact, if you do struggle with hip problems right now, this will change your life. There are two common postures that directly feed sciatica and hip issues (and low back pain). Once you understand how, you can make the necessary changes to support your healing process. If you don't, your physical therapy, trigger point therapy, and adjustments may never actually help long term. Here's why.

STANDING TO ONE SIDE CREATES SCIATICA, HIP, AND LOWER BACK PAIN

You might be like the roughly 95 percent of people I see in my clinic who stand off to one side, placing their weight over the right or left leg, and who feel confused about why they can't seem to get out of pain. Once they understand that their posture directly contributes to their suffering, they set about the simple, but not easy, task of changing how they sit and stand. Postural habits are hard to break but well worth the effort. I cannot stress enough how important it is to attend to your posture.

Recall from the *Sciatica and Trigger Points* chapter that my right hip sat higher than the left. This position kept a constant pull on my outer right hip and gluteus minimus muscle which led to my sciatica symptoms. It also kept the right side of my lower back squashed short which led to trigger points in those low back muscles, the quadratus lumborum specifically. It also led to shortening of my right inner thigh muscles. Standing with my weight to the right reinforced that whole tensional system.

Check out the picture below of Alice standing with her weight off to the right. Can you see her right hip jacked up high? Notice the space between her ribs and pelvis on the right side is smaller (where her hand is on her hip) than that space on the left. Her left hip is dropped lower, which opens up the left side of the waist and low back. This is exactly how I always stood, which led to the misery of chronic sciatica.

When the right hip is pushed off to the right, the gluteus minimus and its best friend, gluteus medius, get weak and full of trigger points. The glute min and glute med are what I call **the rotator cuff of the hip.** One of the jobs of these muscles is to lift the thigh out to the side, hip abduction. Another job of

STANDING ON THE RIGHT

Standing with the weight on the right leg.

those glutes is to stabilize the femur in the hip socket, hence the term *rotator cuff of the hip.* They stabilize the hip joint.

When glute med and min are loaded with trigger points, they struggle to stabilize the hip, causing the hip to be less stable, to feel weak. If you have those trigger points, you may notice that your hip aches or your sciatica symptoms increase during long walks, when you go for a run, or long periods of standing. Glute min and med contract every step you take to keep your hip joint stabilized. Those muscles try real hard to grab that femur and push it back in the socket but they can't do it well because trigger points cause weakness. The hip pushed out to the side pulls on those muscles, removing their leverage, which makes them have to work harder to get the job done. But they can't work harder. They are weak.

The lower back is shorter on one side and longer on the other. This position distorts the TLF and could lead to inflammation, thickening of that fascia, and affect all the other muscles that attach into it. This is a setup for lower back pain along with the sciatica symptoms.

Notice her left foot is turned out. The foot on the side you're not standing on will almost always turn out, shortening the piriformis and other hip rotators on that side. The piriformis on the right is pulled long. Either one may ache and have active trigger points causing piriformis syndrome.

The inner thigh muscles on the right get drawn short and the ones on the left are pulled long as the pelvis tilts up on the right and down on the left. Trigger points in those muscles can lead to groin pain, inner knee pain, even pain inside your pelvis (Travell and Simons 1993).

That postural home felt natural to me. It's where I just kept ending up whenever I checked my standing posture. It took a while to change that habit. I noticed when my pain started to flare up, I was standing, or sitting, with my right hip high. When I shifted, my pain lessened immediately. Standing off to the right wasn't the only culprit. I also fed my sciatica by sitting with my legs crossed.

UNCROSS YOUR LEGS!

Dang, this is a hard one to change. But really important because sitting with your legs crossed is actually wreaking havoc on your body. Take a look at the picture below with Alice sitting with her right leg crossed over her left. Notice that this position pushes her right hip up higher than the left. Sitting this way will create the same issues as standing with the weight over to the right.

Most of the time if someone has a right hip higher than the left, they will sit with the right leg crossed on top. It makes sense because it lands them in the same position as standing on that side. With the right hip up high, the right side of the lower back is shortened while the left hip is dropped low, hanging the left side of the lower back long. Additionally, now both inner thigh groups are pulled short as the knees cross, which can result in both hips becoming weak and achy. Again, the perfect setup for low back and sciatica pain.

SITTING WITH LEGS CROSSED

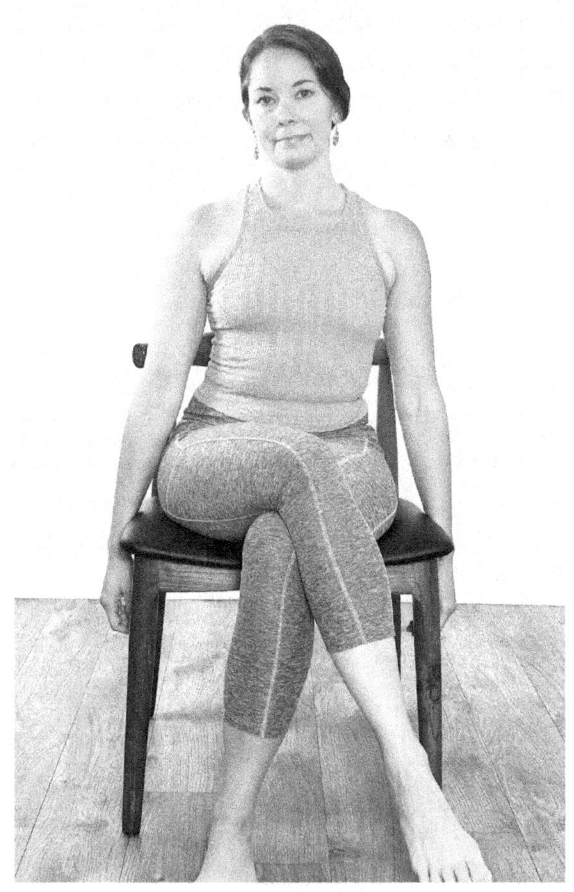

Sitting with the right leg crossed over the left.
Notice how this affects the hips, low back,
neck, and shoulders.

Notice that her torso tilts which puts her ribcage off center, her shoulders land at different heights, and her head leans to the right. This is a setup for neck and shoulder tension, pain, and headaches.

Right now are your legs crossed with one knee over the other? Uncross them. Plant both feet on the floor. If your legs are not long enough for your feet to reach the floor, put something underneath your feet such as a pillow, yoga blocks, or small stool.

Now that you're sitting with your legs uncrossed, are you slouching? Ugh. Another common posture that can lead to chronic pain in the back, and even contribute to issues in the neck, shoulders, and, well, everywhere.

CHAPTER 21

Posture, Sitting, and Back Pain

———

Tracy was a graduate student when she came in to see me for lower back pain. At thirty-one years old, she was determined to finish her degree in social work so she could go out into the world and make a difference helping people to have better lives. She worked a lot at a computer to support herself, then worked at a computer to do her schoolwork. She spent most of her time curled over her laptop, sometimes on the couch and sometimes in bed. Her busy work and school schedule limited her ability to exercise. By the time I met her she was afraid to exercise, worried she would hurt herself more. Had she injured her spine somehow? Would she finish her degree only to be too disabled by this back pain to live out her dreams? Would she ever feel better? These questions plagued her. She was constantly in a stress response.

Tracy feared she'd done some damage to her back and spine. She shared that when she sat to write or study, after a short time her back ached horribly. That pain affected her concentration and ability to work. Sometimes, and more regularly as the days went by, it was difficult to get up from sitting. Once upright, to stand for more than about twenty minutes would trigger her lower back pain. "It seems like no matter what I do, I'm going to be in pain," she told me.

Tracy went to see her doctor to understand her pain, hoping to get relief. Fortunately, the doctor found no signs of damage to her spine. Unfortunately, his "diagnosis" was, "You're just getting old, that's all. Take some Ibuprofen and get used to it." Have you reached this point in your journey? Has someone told you to "get used to it"? Or maybe you yourself have decided it's time for that. It's not. Don't give up yet!

It's a terrible thing to tell someone to just get used to their pain. That's a DIM, Danger In Me. It's ridiculous to tell someone who is thirty-one that she's just getting old. Thirty-one is not old. And it certainly doesn't mean you will be stuck with back pain for the rest of your life. It simply means that her doctor had no idea what to do to help her.

The best a doctor such as Tracy's can do is to let you know that there are no major structural issues with your spine so you can be released to seek other types of support on your healing journey. Most of the time back pain is a warning sign. Your body is trying to protect you from something going really wrong. The body uses pain as a signal to alter how you do things so you don't create a bigger problem. Back pain is often a result of poor sitting posture, trigger points in the muscles, and sticky fascia. Yet most people worry they have a significant disc issue, which we already learned is most often not the cause of the pain.

Tracy's back pain was a direct result of slouching as she worked on her laptop. When you slouch, your upper body takes the shape of forward head posture. The shoulders curl inward and the head drops forward. In the lower body, the pelvis tucks underneath you, the belly and hamstrings shorten, and the back muscles are pulled long. Often the back begins to ache and it may ache relentlessly, like Tracy's did. Her fascia had trapped inflammation and her back muscles kept trying to pull her upright but couldn't do it because they had grown weak from hanging long all the time.

Two muscles that live in the belly cause pain in the back: the rectus abdominis and the psoas. Check out the picture of the pain referral pattern for the rectus abdominis. Notice that this muscle creates an ache across the middle of the back and across the lower back and top of the hips. Does that look like something you have felt in your own body? Remember I said that when you try to sit upright that you may feel an ache in your back? The back muscles can cause that and so can the rectus abdominis. When you try to sit up, the rectus abdominis has to lengthen. If it's got trigger points and you try to sit up, that can activate the trigger points, and lead to either of those pain patterns. When I treated the young boy with back pain, I started our work with techniques to release his belly muscles. Opening the belly muscles and fascia released some of the pull on his back muscles. Once those were softer, I was able to work directly on the back with more success.

RECTUS ABDOMINIS REFERRALS

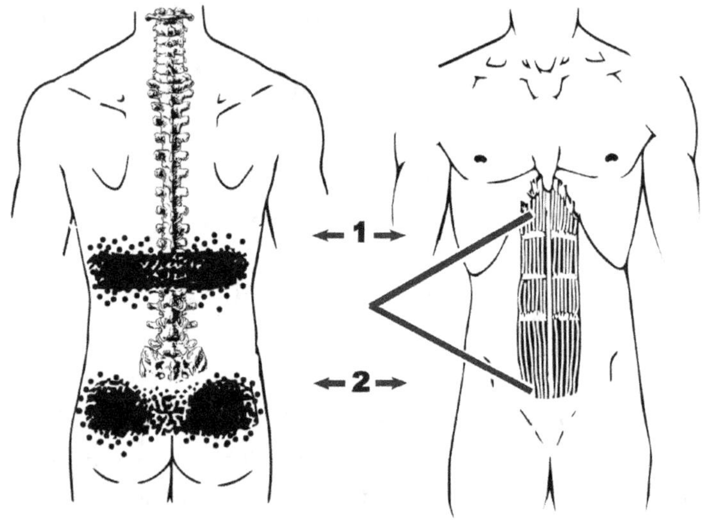

Rectus abdominis can create aching across the middle back or across the top of the pelvis and sacrum/very lower back area.

BACK TO THE PSOAS

Fear seems to go hand-in-hand with lower back pain. As we discussed in the *Stress* section, fear is going to directly impact the psoas, causing it to contract and grip the lower spine. The psoas will strongly contract when we are afraid, as a mode of protection. If you are chronically sitting in a slouched posture, the psoas will get shortened, pulling on the lumbar spine and creating lower back pain. So now we've got two things that are shortening the psoas: slouched sitting and worry about the pain.

When the psoas is stuck short, it will resist lengthening, which it must do for you to stand up straight without pain, just like the rectus abdominis. This is what happened to Tracy. When she tried to stand up after working on her laptop, her back hurt up and down her lumbar spine. She became stressed and worried about having back pain, which further contracted her psoas muscle and contributed to her pain. She was in a vicious cycle of pain, worry about the pain, then more pain. Travell and Simons make it clear that a muscle that is held in a shortened position, especially while contracted, is more likely to have active trigger points (Travell, Simons, and Simons, 1999). When you sit, your hip flexors are shortened. If you experience stress when you sit, like with the pressures of your work for instance, those muscles will also be contracted as part of the stress response: a recipe for activating trigger points.

Once Tracy understood that her posture was the cause of her back pain, she became dedicated to changing it. She moved from the couch to a table to work on her laptop. She got a good, sturdy chair to make it easier to sit well. In a short time, while using the other parts of the FreeBody Method, she was able to get rid of her back pain for good.

I'd like to speak to studies that have come out that found no correlation between sitting for work and back pain. One review paper looked at a multitude of previous studies and found no correlation to sitting and lower back pain (Roffey et al. 2010). They report, "It is unlikely that occupational sitting is independently causative of LBP (lower back pain) in the populations of workers studied." In my research, I found studies that linked posture and sitting to lower back pain and studies that rebuked those links.

My interpretation is that if you don't have lower back pain, or neck pain for that matter, it's fine to slouch on the couch *sometimes*. But if you do have some trigger points in the muscles that are held shortened, such as the hip flexors, those trigger points might become more active from long periods of sitting, especially in a slouched posture. The muscles that are pulled long often have trigger points. When you slouch, your back muscles are pulled long. Trigger points in those muscles will activate over time.

Your position becomes your posture, and your posture becomes trained into the tissues. Posture is a long-haul issue, meaning over time, and perhaps many years. Muscles that are held short and long become ingrained that way. This explains why short-term studies may not truly reflect the cost of poor posture. The fact that you may, and probably *do*, have latent trigger points at the least, means that you will, over time, reinforce those patterns and activate some trigger points out of their latency, resulting in pain.

Luke's head was dropped forward for many years, and over time, his forward head posture became ingrained in the tissues and affected the shape of his spine, limiting his ability to bring his head back over his shoulders. He experiences regular neck pain partly because he can no longer pull his head back over his shoulders. He cannot, to a large enough degree, alter the position of his head and neck. His trigger points continue to be burdensome. His fascia continues to be thick and unyielding. Yet, he has improved and experiences less pain than before.

My hope is that you will read this and think about the long-term implications of the posture you most often find yourself in. Are you slouching? Is your head forward of your shoulders? Are you looking down at your phone or laptop a lot during the day? If yes, I encourage you to make the effort it takes to establish good posture habits. It takes some time but once you have good posture trained into your body, it becomes effortless.

In the next section you will learn the Five Points of Freedom of the FreeBody Method. Good posture is one of those points and you will learn techniques to get yourself into good posture. But first, let me introduce you to FreeBody.

PART 5

FREEBODY

CHAPTER 22

The FreeBody System: The 5 Points of Freedom

We have laid the foundation for what systems are essential to pain or the absence of pain: trigger points in muscles, sticky fascia, and stress in the brain. We learned posture can be a big piece of the pain puzzle and how it relates to those three. I will now introduce you to the FreeBody System.

The FreeBody System is based on an understanding that to really get out of pain, assuming there is no underlying disease or chronically poor diet (that's another book entirely and not my expertise), you must attend to five key things: Breath and the Brain, Posture, Movement, Stretching, and Therapeutic Rolling. Therapeutic Rolling is both Self-Myofascial Release (SMFR) and Self-Trigger-Point Release (STPR). SMFR helps to hydrate and free the fascia. STPR takes care of the trigger points you already have while the other Four Points of Freedom keep them from returning or developing. If all the FreeBody Five Points of Freedom are attended to, you have the greatest opportunity to get out of pain, reduce the effects of aging, and keep pain at bay.

You will learn how to care for your body so you can feel your best, no matter what age you are. Really. I've witnessed people in their seventies and eighties release pain they've had for decades and get back to things they believed they couldn't do any more. Hooray! There's so much discomfort that you don't have to live with. With a little bit of regular attention throughout the day, your body can feel amazing.

I have worked with thousands of people over my thirty-year career. I get to help people out of pain every single day. Once I implemented this whole approach to pain relief, I saw my clients shift dramatically and quickly. Now is the time. Let's do this. Check out www.FreeBodyBook.com for tons of resources and videos to support your journey. Welcome home to your body, to your FreeBody.

CHAPTER 23

Freedom Point #1: Soothe Your Brain

Earlier in the book, I shared some simple practices to tame the Inner Neanderthal so you can reduce stress throughout your day. Recall that I spoke about belly breathing and also shaking out your body as some key practices for stress reduction. Belly breathing, pushing your belly out as you breathe in deeply, sends that signal to your brain that you feel safe. Shaking out your body helps to process some of the stress chemistry building up in your system. It also serves to soften your fascia, increase hydration, and relax your muscles. Great practices!

Some people struggle with focusing on the breath. It causes them more anxiety. I have worked with folks with panic disorder, anxiety, and chronic stress for several years and often they find that moving first is a better approach for them. Wonderful! Sometimes you have to speed your body up to meet the epinephrine (adrenaline) rushing through it. You speed up to slow down. You will naturally slow down after a while and your energy will be more settled, less fight-or-flight oriented. If you get more anxious by focusing on your breath, try a moving practice instead, such as Fake Running. Here's how that works.

FAKE RUNNING

Get into a runners stance, crouched down with one foot behind you as if you're about to take off in a run, because you sort of are about to do that. Clench your fists, look forward, and then pump your arms really fast, pretending to run but not moving your legs. Go! See whatever stressful situation is at hand getting smaller behind you. You always win! Mad at your boss or work? Fake run away! Dealing with a difficult moment in your relationship? Get outta there! In imagination of course. Pump those arms, imagine you are running through the woods, on a track, or wherever it feels good for you to imagine to be. Pump your arms hard and fast. Get yourself going. Every once in a while, switch legs, putting the front leg behind you and the back leg in front. I like to jump to do this. It's really fun and a bit silly, but an incredibly effective way to process stress chemistry and to see yourself winning and getting to safety.

After a couple of minutes of that, start to slow it down. Tell yourself, "I am safe." Come up to stand tall. Stretch your arms overhead and reach long and tall to the sky. Bring your hands down slowly, perhaps folded over your heart, and take a few long slow deep breaths, focusing on the exhale. You can exhale through puffed cheeks.

Last fall, I was hired by a global corporation to work with an international group of human resource team leaders. I was asked to teach them about stress, resilience, and ways to keep their teams on track with stress reduction strategies. One of this group's favorite practices was the Fake Running practice. It's a great way to move energy and allow your body to experience the "flight" part. We were all laughing together as we "ran" in the conference room. At the end, many said they would use this practice for decompressing their nervous systems. I recommended their whole team do it together when things got difficult. If you're a manager or team leader, the next time your group is struggling to solve a problem and everyone is getting tense, why not try Fake Running as a way to blow off steam? You'll be surprised how well this works.

KEEP A JOY JOURNAL

I counsel my clients to keep a joy journal to remind their brains what joy feels like. The more you use any part of your brain, the easier it is to use that part of your brain. Reinforce the joy networks by remembering joy you have had in the past. Write down those stories in as much detail as possible. When you feel upset or hurt and need to shift your mental state, pull out your Joy Journal and read it.

MAKE A FUN FRAME

You know those picture frames with spaces for a bunch of photos? Get one of those. Print a bunch of pictures of you on a fun vacation, with someone you love, on that zip line you did that one time, at a friend's party, and make yourself a Fun Frame. Hang it up where it's easy to see to remind yourself that you *do* have fun, that you remember feeling good. The Fun Frame is the same idea as the Joy Journal. Remind yourself that there are good times and activate the joy networks.

I interviewed a long-time massage therapist and friend, Althea Wilkins. When I asked her if there was anything she'd recommend to help folks feel better in their bodies and lives she said, "Have more fun! Enjoy your life!" Yes, Althea. Yes.

BREATHING PRACTICE: COOLING THE SOUP BREATH

Once you have more control over your nervous system, working with the breath is the fastest way out of stress. Modern science is now proving what the yogis of old knew all along: to get peaceful and calm you need to lengthen your exhale and slow down your breath. When you breathe with a longer exhale relative to the inhale, you communicate directly with your vagus nerve and shift out of a stress response (Komori 2018).

A practice I learned at Kripalu in Yoga Therapy school is called "cooling the soup breath." It's a super easy way to get your exhale longer and slower. Here's how to do it.

Imagine you have a hot bowl of soup in front of you and you really want to eat it but it's too hot. You take a spoonful up to your mouth. How do you cool it down? You purse your lips and slowly blow over the top of it, not too hard or fast or you'll blow the soup off the spoon, right? That's basically how to do this breathing practice. You simply imagine you have a spoonful of hot soup in front of your mouth, purse your lips, and blow over it, long and slow. Do this three to five times. Notice how you feel. Better? Yeah. You don't even have to wait until you notice you are stressing out. Just do this a couple of times a day.

Here's something important I want to say to you that I wish someone had said to me. If you are in a situation, work or personal relationship, and you are *having* to self-regulate all the time, having to navigate stress all the damn time, maybe you need to reevaluate the environment you are in. Self-regulation is important, sure. But if you're having to do it all the time, well, life just isn't meant to be that stressful. We humans seem to get habituated to high stress levels, and that's not really serving us. If you were raised in a stressful environment, your brain might be thinking that your current stressful environment is normal. What is familiar has a certain safety about it. I personally have traded actual safety for that little bit of false safety, the comfortable familiar, by staying with the known danger. We humans do it all the time. But we don't have to. We can live better lives! If it is possible to change your situation, consider how that could be done. Get help if you need. Then once you're out, you'll need a NERP to deal with the mental consequences of being in that stressful environment all the time. A NERP is my term which means a Neural Emotional Reprogramming Practice. Let me explain.

SPECIAL PRACTICE FOR TRAUMA: NERPS

If you have experienced a trauma, you know what I mean when I say that it is a real challenge to get that out of your head. If you've ever been in a relationship with someone who was manipulative or had a lot of narcissistic traits, you have experienced ruminating. Ruminating is when you can't stop thinking about the bad person or situation. Every time you think of it, your brain believes it is happening right then and you get worked up. Heart races, blood pumps, fists engage, the whole thing. Remember Natalie who came to me with tons of trigger points but the real problem was that she was stuck in protection mode from physical abuse? That's a result of ruminating. She couldn't stop being worried that she was in danger. She couldn't stop thinking about the abuse. This caused her to be in pain all the time.

If you're worried about your physical pain and you can't stop thinking about it, and keep getting more afraid, that's a kind of ruminating. If you keep being worried that *something is really wrong in there*, that fear is feeding your pain. Remember that worrying about your pain is a DIM, Danger In Me. Your pain will lessen when you stop ruminating about how much pain you have, or how sickly your body might be. Stop catastrophizing your pain. Maybe the pain is actually a response to the fear about the pain. Hmm...

I shared earlier that I experienced PTSD after I left a particularly difficult relationship. I thought about that person nearly every single second and rage boiled inside me. I couldn't believe I had been taken advantage of and that I had stayed as long as I had. I felt shame. I decided really early on that I would not stay that way. I knew I could not live with that level of stress and anger.

To get free, I had to stop ruminating. I had to stop obsessively thinking about that person and the terrible ways I had been betrayed. To do that, I created a NERP: Neural Emotional Reprogramming Practice. The idea is that you have to stop thinking about the bad thing and think about something good instead. Yeah, right. *Ha*! But it works. Slowly at first. Every time you change your thoughts, you win! You are re-training your brain, re-wiring your brain for joy. It's a beautiful thing. In the beginning, you might have to change your thoughts every single minute. But then it's every five minutes. Then a half hour. Then days, weeks, and months. It gets better. Whew.

Here's an example. Early in the process, I could barely drive to work because I got so angry. Every time I saw a vehicle that looked like his (why did suddenly *everyone* drive that kind of vehicle?) I would literally start yelling terrible things out loud. The vehicle was a trigger, something that put me right back into those terrible memories, feelings, and hatred. I would not hate. I would not succumb to it because it was ruining my life almost as bad as staying in the relationship itself would have. Because in a way, I was still in it.

Whenever I saw a vehicle like his, instead of yelling obscenities, I started yelling, "Congratulations on your success, Cat! You're doing a great job!" And then I would call to mind a good memory. I picked one when I was dancing with my dear nephew, James. I would picture one particular night that was really fun. I said, "Dance and be free for all the world to see." It's good if it rhymes as that's easier to remember. I pictured us dancing and laughing, reminded myself what joy felt like.

It totally worked. After about a week, I no longer got upset when I saw that type of car. Cool, right? It works even better if you can do some kind of body movement with it, like throwing your arms up in the air as if in victory. Bringing the body into it helps to connect more parts of your brain.

To create a NERP, write down a positive memory. Make it a statement such as "I feel good when I hike in the woods," or something like that, which represents your positive memory. Write down a description of that actual joyful event to go with it, perhaps a particular night out or a hike to a beautiful waterfall. Recall as much as you can. What color was the sky or the lights? What were the sounds? Were you eating? What did the food taste like? Can you feel the sun on your face or the heat of your body from dancing? Embellish it as much as possible.

Then make up a physical movement to go with it. I had one for in the car which was shaking my right arm around. When I was standing and a negative thought would come, I would kick and do a dance move and say, "Dance and be free for all the world to see." I danced around for a moment, reliving that actual joyful memory with as many embellished details as I could muster. I saw my friends smiling. I laughed with my nephew James. I heard the music. I saw the lights and the band. Eventually, I stopped thinking about that guy completely. I didn't have to use the NERP any longer because I was no longer ruminating. Use a tool until you no longer need it. The idea is be as healed as possible, not in a perpetual state of healing. Then new tools emerge to support the next phase of your journey, whatever that may be.

REWIRE YOUR BRAIN OUT OF HYPERVIGILANCE

Harvard has produced many great studies on the effects of meditation and mindfulness on the brain and body. In 2011, Harvard researchers released a study in which they scanned the brains of participants before and after they entered an eight-week meditation program. These brain scans proved unquestionably that we can, in fact, *change our brains structurally* with meditation in as little as eight weeks. Participants reported an average of twenty-seven minutes a day following guided meditation practices.

At the end of the study, scientists found two very interesting results in the brain scans relative to gray matter. Gray matter is the stuff in your brain that supports the processing of information related to memory, emotions, and movement. Deterioration of gray matter means that information cannot be processed as readily, as is found in people with dementia and stroke victims who have lost gray matter as a result. Less gray matter means the affected part of the brain cannot work as well (Mercadante and Tadi 2022).

In this study they found "increased gray-matter density in the hippocampus, known to be important for learning and memory, and in structures associated with self-awareness, compassion, and introspection." What that means is that the parts of your brain that support higher emotions, such as compassion, could operate more efficiently and process greater amounts of information. This is what we would expect from meditation, right? Meditators appear more calm, more kind, and more empathetic.

Here's where it got really interesting to me. The Harvard researchers also found that the gray matter density around the *amygdala* noticeably shrank. What that means is that the alarm system wasn't quite as trigger happy, pun intended. The participants reported reductions in stress. Meditation structurally changes your brain to reduce your triggers. That's amazing.

You can heal! You can get out of hypervigilance and reduce your pain significantly. Your brain can literally and structurally change in just eight weeks of following *guided* meditations. You don't even need to know how to meditate. You can simply download one of the incredible free meditation apps that are readily available (I use the Insight Timer) and within eight weeks, your brain will change.

I GET IT... MY VERSION OF "IT" ANYWAY

I know how hard it is to experience a traumatic event, childhood, or relationship. I know it's hard to let it be and move on. That's the trickiest part of trauma. It takes over your brain, your thoughts, steals your joy, and may be causing you all kinds of pain. Trauma is a chronic stress response which puts your body on guard. It may be a root cause of your pain and suffering. I'm here to tell you that you don't have to let it. Make the NERP and use it. Follow guided meditations. Make a Joy Journal and Fun Frame. You can do it! You can get free. Freedom is exquisite.

*Reminder that the book website has a bunch of videos and information to support your healing practices. Check them out. I have included a free Introduction to Meditation and Self-Regulation Course on there. I'm happy to help you at www.FreeBodyBook.com

CHAPTER 24

Freedom Point #2: Active Posture

SO WHAT IS GOOD POSTURE?

We covered a lot about posture already and I know you are motivated to take care of your body in this way. So what *is* good posture anyway? If I ask you to imagine someone in poor posture, you'll probably visualize someone slouching, shoulders rounded forward, and their body curled inward. You got it! Don't do that. It's important to hold yourself up when you sit and to stand without leaning on something. Why is everyone leaning on the wall, the counter, or the shopping cart at the grocery store? Our bodies are designed to hold us up and we needn't collapse into the couch or counter all the time. In fact, this will contribute to weakness in key muscles which are designed to hold you upright. When I speak to my clients about "good posture" I call it **Active Posture** because there is an element of lifting oneself up toward the sky. In the website for this book there is a section on posture training with links of videos to follow.

Below I will give you some cues to find your way into Active Posture.

ACTIVE POSTURE STANDING

Here's that picture of Alice standing in good posture again. See her ears are over her shoulders which are over her hips.

GOOD POSTURE

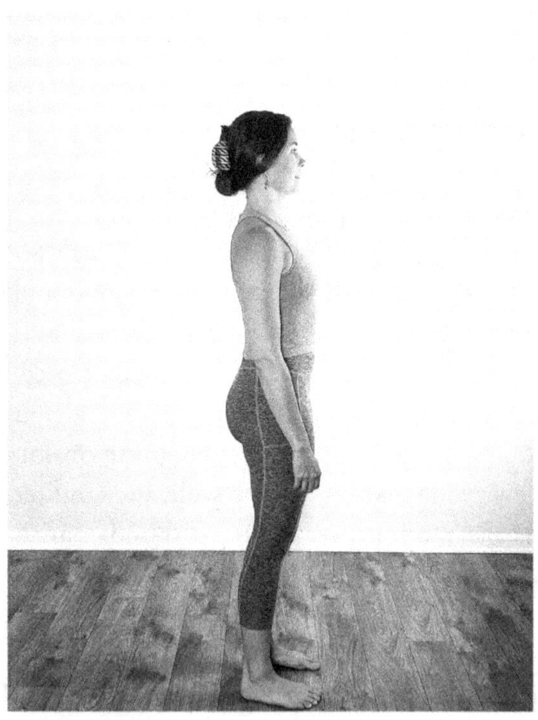

Good posture. Ears over shoulders over
hips over ankles.

Her hips are over her ankles. Optimal position! Here is a step-by-step walkthrough.

- Stand tall with your feet hip distance apart.
- Lift your chest and let your head rest over your shoulders, not in front of them.
- Avoid overarching your back by bringing your awareness to the back of your body and lift the back of your ribs up a little. Imagine lifting the entire ribcage: front, sides, and back together.
- Reach the crown of your head toward the sky, as if pushing a button with the top of your head. This is the active part which also serves to decompress the spine.
- Keep your chin level with the floor.
- When you stop to talk with someone, stay standing tall. Resist the temptation to lean on the wall or counter.

ACTIVE POSTURE SITTING

- When sitting, slide yourself toward the front of a firm chair so your butt is on the chair but your thighs are not.
- Uncross your legs and plant your feet on the floor (or other support) with your knees hip distance apart.
- Sit up tall with your head over your shoulders and your shoulders over your hips.
- Untuck your pelvis. Don't allow your chest and belly to collapse inward.
- Reach the crown of your head toward the sky, as if pushing a button with the top of your head. This is the active part which also serves to decompress the spine.
- Remember to breathe.

I worked with a client who ran a landscaping business in the town where he used to live, three-and-a-half hours away. He drove to check on his clients and team twice a week. When he first came in, he said he couldn't drive more than thirty minutes without terrible pain in his lower back. I asked him about his driving position and discovered that he was slouched with his pelvis tucked under as he drove. Car seats are terrible and often foster slouched posture. I recommended that he place a rolled towel underneath his butt to elevate his hips a little and help to tilt his pelvis forward out of the tucked position. This would stop his back muscles from being chronically pulled long and relieve some of the shortening in the belly and hamstrings.

It worked! The next time I saw him, he reported that the best thing to relieve his back pain in the car was that little towel under his butt. He realized the next time he was driving that three-and-a-half hours, he was almost to his destination before he had to stop. He went from about thirty minutes of driving without pain to three hours! This speaks volumes of the power of posture when you've got trigger points and sticky fascia. He then went about following the steps to release his trigger points for lasting relief. His efforts were effective in part because he did not keep activating them with his driving posture.

Now here's the kicker. No posture, no matter how active and perfect it looks, is perfect for long. At some point, you must get up and move because our bodies are designed for movement, not stillness. We are not meant to sit all day in *any* position. Some folks are using standing desks these days which can be great, unless you stand at your desk in your habitual poor posture. While the standing desk can be helpful, moving around is more beneficial. When I have long periods of work to do on a computer, I switch between standing, using my bike desk, and sitting. We must move regularly. Let's talk about movement next.

CHAPTER 25

Freedom Point #3: Move

"Sitting is the new smoking."

—DR. JAMES LEVINE, DIRECTOR OF THE MAYO
CLINIC AT ARIZONA STATE UNIVERSITY

If you are one of those people who now sits for much of the workday, there are many reasons to get up and move around. Serious reasons. The Mayo Clinic looked at thirteen studies of people and their activity levels and "they found that those who sat for more than eight hours a day with no physical activity had a risk of dying similar to that posed by obesity and smoking" (Laskowski 2022).

Whoa. That's a big deal. So yes, sitting *is* the new smoking.

Sitting for too long is bad for your health. It's bad for your heart, your blood pressure, your insulin levels, and just about every system in your body. It's also bad for your joints, connective tissues, and muscles. So how does sitting for prolonged periods of time cause soft tissue problems, joint dysfunction, and pain?

In the *Posture* section, we discussed how sitting in the wrong posture can affect the muscles and fascia as well as your experience in your body, perhaps leading to tension and pain in a variety of areas in your body. But what if you're sitting in great posture, in active posture? Isn't that better?

Well, yes and no. Sitting in active posture is certainly an improvement over sitting slumped at your desk or table or, even worse, crouched over your laptop on the couch. Yet, the problem with sitting too much is not simply about the *position* that you're sitting in. It's also about the *stillness*.

STILLNESS CREATES STIFFNESS. MOTION IS LOTION.

Chronic stillness is not good. It dehydrates the tissues and the joints, weakens our muscles, dries out the fascia, and basically leads to a host of pain and dysfunction in the body. In an ideal situation, about two thirds of the volume of fascia is made up of water (Magown 2017). It is movement that flushes the joints and keeps the fascial tissues, muscles, and the spaces between the muscles, hydrated. When the tissues and joints are dehydrated, they cannot function optimally. When they aren't functioning properly, range of motion is lost, and pain can set up camp.

Recall that in the *Fascia* section I said that if you don't move enough your fascia isn't staying hydrated because it is movement that makes the tissues call for fluids. When there is less fluid in your fascia, it thickens because there are more fibers relative to the amount of fluid. We discussed those collagen fibers knitting together in adhesions. This further dehydrates the tissues, binding you up. We have to move around to generate the demand for water in the tissues. When you sit still for too long, your Jell-O starts to get thicker, your collagen sticks together, and you lose the ability to move as much as you did yesterday. Over time, this gets worse.

When I spoke to Gil Hedley, he said, "the sliding surfaces of the muscles, the fascial bags, are meant to slide on one another and they do so because they are living in water. No water, no slide. No slide equals loss of movement." So not only do big sheets of fascia, like that thoracolumbar fascia, dry and get stuck together, but your actual muscles can get stuck together as well. Your fascia really wants you to move a whole lot.

The next question is, how does dehydration affect our muscles directly, besides their fascial bags getting stuck together?

There have been many studies that show that dehydration has a negative effect on cardiovascular exercise. The muscles cannot function optimally partly because the heart is having to work really hard to pump oxygen to them. Less fluid means less blood means the heart has to work really hard to get enough blood, and therefore oxygen, to nourish the muscles. Less fluid in the fascia means that the vascular pathways, the fascia spaces through which the blood vessels travel, get thicker, making it harder for the blood to get through. It's kind of like trying to water your garden with a hose that's kinked, so there's more of a trickle than a flow. Dehydrated sticky fascia crimps your blood hoses, which means that your muscles can't get all the nourishment they need.

How does dehydration effect the ability of muscles to do non-cardiovascular work? Does a loss of hydration affect our strength?

In 2008, a study was conducted to see if dehydration had an effect on anaerobic muscular contraction. Anaerobic contraction doesn't require oxygen to get nutrients to the tissues. It's the opposite of a cardio workout. Anaerobic activities include weightlifting or lifting your kids. The results of the study concluded that with a 2.9 percent level of dehydration there was about a 7 percent decrease in strength in the upper body and an almost 20 percent decrease in strength in the lower body. The subjects fatigued an average of 70 percent more quickly (Jones et al. 2008). That's huge! Just a little bit of dehydration caused the subjects to tire far more quickly.

What this study teaches is that we become less capable of doing the things we need to do in our lives, like carry groceries and laundry and children, the less hydrated we are. We fatigue faster. We get tired. Neither our muscles nor fascia can work properly and then we move even less. Then less movement, more dehydration, less movement…

You can drink water all day long but if you don't move, you're not moving that water through your body, you're not telling your body to demand more water, and you're just going to pee it out. Have you ever had that experience? You keep drinking water, but you still feel dehydrated and you keep peeing it all out? It might be partly due to stress, but it might also be because you're too still. Movement pushes the fluids through your body, between your muscles, and through your fascia.

MOVEABLE JOINTS AND FLUID

Joints are places in the body where bones come together. In the joints that move, each has a capsule surrounding the ends of the bones that create the joint. This capsule is filled with a slippery fluid called synovial fluid and the capsule is called the synovial capsule.

Synovial fluid nourishes the slippery cartilage that covers the ends of the bones. Cartilage is that stuff that keeps the hard ends of the bones from grinding on each other. If you've ever experienced a cartilage injury or loss of cartilage, you know the pain of grinding bones is awful.

Synovial fluid protects the cartilage by acting as a shock absorber and it keeps your bones from crashing into each other. Swimming around in your synovial fluid are the cells of repair, called fibroblasts, and the cells of inflammation which will be activated if there is harm or injury to the joint. Cartilage is avascular, which means it does not have its own blood supply. Cartilage relies on synovial fluid to remove its waste. If there's not enough fluid in the joint, waste products can accumulate and render the joint less functional, even painful.

Synovial fluid is generated by the synovial membrane, which is the inner lining of the joint capsule. That membrane responds to your movement demands by producing more synovial fluid because your body says, "Hey, this person wants this joint to move so I better keep enough fluid in there to keep things healthy and keep the bones from grinding on each other." Sure, a little synovial fluid will be generated even when you are sitting still. But movement stimulates the synovial membrane to produce much more fluid, which then in turn further supports the cartilage and the joints. If you're not moving, you're making far less synovial fluid and your joints suffer, the cartilage suffers, and then movement suffers. Without enough fluids in your joints, your cartilage wears down and your joints get full of waste products, which can hurt. If you want to keep joints like your knees hydrated and happy, you must move.

One last point about fascia, pain, and movement comes from a lecture I watched with Victoria L. Magown of MyoRehab in Albuquerque, New Mexico. She said that "Fascia likes to be busy! You've got to move it or it gets very unhappy. It tightens up and you're in pain." She went on to say that, "Fascia goes searching for pain with a magnifying glass" (2017). Don't let your fascia sit idle. Give it some movement to play with.

So now you might be asking, how much and how often should I move?

BORN TO MOVE

If you are a fan of the gym, or a morning run or exercise routine, you might be thinking that this doesn't apply to you. It *does* apply to you if, after you exercise, you go and sit for the rest of the day. Just moving a bunch at one point in the day is not going to keep you hydrated for the whole day. Remember that you're filled with Jell-O. As Jell-O sits, it sets. It solidifies. As you sit, your tissues immediately begin to lose hydration. You start to set like the Jell-O. We have to move regularly throughout the day to keep up the demand for water in our bodies, to keep our tissues soft and slickery. We were born to move, designed to move. We've got arms and shoulders built for climbing. We've got legs built for walking and running...and dancing. Dancing is just the best movement because, at least the way I do it, you can move any which way you want.

To get all your tissues hydrated in all directions, you need to move all your parts through their full range of motion regularly. Gil Hedley said to me that we've got to move differently than our normal ways because "our social movements are a straitjacket." He means that we become imprisoned by the same old forward and backward motions. We need to wiggle, we need to move every part in every direction that we can. That's me on the dance floor.

Remember I said I'd get back to how to free up a thick and matted thoracolumbar fascia? Well this is it. Movement. And massage. Get lots of gliding massage on the TLF and perhaps some myofascial release work. You can do some of that yourself, which you'll learn about in the last chapter.

MOVEMENT BREAK IDEAS

I tell my clients to get up every half hour and just move for a few minutes. You don't really want to go more than an hour without moving. Use the movement breaks to build strength to keep your muscles and fascia healthy. You don't need to do a big workout every day, just move throughout the day, and strengthen while you move.

Try these:

- Start your day with a ten-minute walk, outside if that's available.
- The next time you go to the bathroom, do three to five pushups.
- The next time you put your phone down, get down on the floor on your back, knees bent and feet on the floor, and drop your knees side to side, a.k.a. windshield wipers.
- Stand beside your chair, hand on the chair for support as needed, stand on one leg, and swing the other forward and back behind you.
- Before dinner, have a five-minute dance party in your bedroom.
- Do squats while you brush your teeth.
- Put on your favorite music and dance around, moving your body parts through their ranges of motion.
- Stew Wild tells his clients to get up from their chair and lift their chair up over their heads to activate bigger muscles than they use to sit and type. I keep hand weights nearby and lift those overhead a few times a day.

Movement breaks hydrate and strengthen. At FreeBody, we use the Pomodoro app to remind us to get up and get going.

POMODORO FOR THE WIN!

Pomodoro is a free timer app that allows twenty-five minutes for productivity, then five minutes for a break. You can change those settings as you need. During that five-minute break, you get up from your seat and do some leg swings, dance around a bit, anything to get you moving. Move different parts of your body throughout the day over the breaks. After several rounds of Pomodoro, you get a longer fifteen-minute break. That's a great time to go for walk, swing your arms, and shake your body out. At the end of this section, I give you a sample FreeBody day with movement breaks factored in. Alternatively, you can just do one short movement break every time you go to the bathroom or put down your phone, linking it with something you already do all day anyway.

We instituted the Pomodoro timer at my clinic and it's wonderful! We have discovered that taking these regular breaks actually significantly improved our productivity. Sometimes I walk into the office and there is my assistant rolling on a ball or stretching. It's wonderful! Sometimes we have dance party breaks. We'll turn the music up and dance and bounce around the office. We don't look at social media, we move. Dance party breaks have the added benefit of fun, it lightens up the day and helps us to be in good spirits, especially when things are stressful or there's a deadline looming. Remember that movement is a way to process stress chemistry. Our movement breaks reduce compounded stress during the day, bring us joy together, and keep us hydrated. Try it at your office. Really.

If you need more ideas about movement breaks, I have a bunch for you at www.FreeBodyBook.com. You'll find one-to-two-minute movement breaks to take throughout your day to keep your legs, hips, back, shoulders, and neck from getting stuck.

Moving your body throughout your day is essential to feeling well. Get up and dance. Do some strengthening for one minute. Do some range of motion for one minute. Just get up and move. Nothing replaces movement. There is not one simple fix you can do at the end of a long day of sitting, or standing, to erase all the *stillness* out of your body. *Stillness creates stiffness. Motion is lotion.*

CHAPTER 26

Freedom Point #4: Stretch

I have been practicing yoga for about thirty-five years and teaching it for more than twenty. I have owned two yoga studios, taught in a school of massage and yoga, and taught in many yoga teacher trainings, even one that I created myself and ran for a few years. Yoga is an incredible systematic way to move and stretch your body in all directions. Robert Schleip, the fascia researcher, can be found on many yoga podcasts explaining the great benefits of yoga for the fascia. Stretching is good for fascia.

One of the crown jewels of a good yoga practice is that it stretches full lines of fascia, not just a muscle here or one over there. If you've had sciatica issues and have been stretching your piriformis ad nauseum, you know that's not going to work. Partly because it may not be your piriformis at all that's causing your pain and partly because no muscle works in a vacuum. You can't stretch one part and affect the whole fascial line.

Let me briefly explain fascial lines. Tom Myers in his book, *Anatomy Trains,* describes various tracks of fascia and their muscular counterparts, each portion affecting and pulling on every other portion of the track. For instance, his superficial back line begins at the plantar fascia at the bottom of the foot and runs up along the superficial muscles and sheets of fascia in the calves, thighs, and back, including the thoracolumbar fascia, ending at the base of the skull. In this way of looking at the body, the plantar fascia at the bottom of the foot is directly connected to and related to the trapezius muscle which covers much of the upper back, shoulder region, and back of the neck. Plantar fasciitis anyone? Maybe you need to not just focus on your foot. Myers proposes that to have a positive effect in one area of an Anatomy Train, you need to address all the parts of that continuous stream of tissue, or train track (Myers 2001).

Through this lens we see why yoga is an excellent stretching program because many yoga stretches work across the entire body, opening up the full length of the fascial tracks, and offering a complete system of stretching. Try yoga! One of the problems I regularly see in my clients and students is that they get stuck trying to just stretch one muscle, group of muscles, or area of their body. They say, "My back is tight" and they're just stretching out their back but it doesn't often improve that way. I almost always find they stretch the wrong part. They stretch the part that feels tight. Now bear with me, I know you are thinking, "Well, that makes sense." It sort of does until you understand the difference between tight and taut.

When I spoke with Amber Davies we discussed this. She also observed that many of her clients stretched the opposite side of what they should be stretching. They stretched the tissues that were locked long instead of the ones that were stuck short. Let me give you an example.

When Tracy the graduate student came to see me for her back pain, she had been stretching her back to no avail. I explained to her that, due to her slouching and being stuck in a tuck while sitting all day, her back muscles were already too long. What Schleip helped us to understand is that long muscles are weak and their fascial bags can become weak. If you stretch muscles that are already long and somewhat frail, your body is going to try to protect that tissue from tearing by contracting those muscles or sending you a big pain signal. This is especially true with a loaded stretch, which means hanging your weight on the muscle you are stretching as in a standing forward fold trying to touch your toes. Remember pain is protection. This is why attempting to touch your toes while standing may not feel good in your back.

Nearly everyone that comes to me with back pain talks about stretching their back, and it pretty much never works. They get tighter and they still have pain. I explain to them that they need to open the front body more than the back body. They need to get themselves into positions that stretch open the belly and the chest and they need to actually strengthen the back. This is why core strengthening for back pain often backfires, in my experience. I see people doing all kinds of crunches and sit-ups, which further rounds them forward, tucks their pelvis under, and exacerbates the problem.

I worked with a doctor once, another guy who leaned over an operating table his entire career just like Luke the vet. His back had bothered him for over ten years before he ended up in my office. When I met him, he was doing nearly two hours of physical therapy and yoga therapy every day. He was committed! When I looked at what he was doing, most of it was "strengthening his core" and stretching his back. No wonder he wasn't getting better. I told him to use a soft ball and roll out his belly (I'll get into more detail about therapeutic rolling in the next chapter) to release the front of his body and to strengthen the back of it. That's it. Fifteen minutes a day. You need to *lengthen what's short and strengthen what's long.* About a month later he retired and went hiking in Patagonia with his wife. He later reported it was as if he'd never had back pain at all. After ten years.

The simple understanding that what you feel as *tight* is actually typically something that is pulled *taut* will change your life. Seriously. Taut is what happens to a rubber band when you pull it. The skin of a balloon is stretched taut when it is full of air. Your muscles and fascia are taut when they are pulled long. They often ache because, as I mentioned earlier, tissues don't like being pulled long because they get weaker and their fascial bags get thinner. It's risky. There is danger of tearing and injury. Your brain responds with *protection*: inflammation and pain.

The best way to stretch is to start on the opposite side of what's hurting. If your hips ache, stretch your inner thighs by sitting on the floor with your legs opened wide. If your back aches, open your belly and chest. If the back of your neck aches, open your chest and throat. If your hamstrings ache, stretch your quads. This is just a starting point. The best way is to stretch those full lines of fascia. Yoga does this beautifully. A sun salutation each morning, which I teach through videos on my website, will get you moving while opening the front and back of your body. Add in some side bends and a twist and you'll have almost all the parts. I want to remind you that we need to move through our full range of motion to keep things hydrated, not just front, back, and side to side.

As Gil Hedley said, "We need to move outside of our culturally accepted ways of moving. You need to get a little weird with your movement." *Yes*! That's why I love dancing. It moves you around in all directions through all ranges of movement. Well, it *can* anyway, if you dance like I do. You know, kinda weird and all over the place.

SOME CAUTION FOR YIN YOGA PRACTICE

I'd like to make a point about Yin yoga, which will get me into trouble with those that like it. Yin yoga is a style of yoga where you get into a stretch and stay there as long as ten minutes. Whoa. I've seen a lot of people get injured with Yin yoga. Actually, I've seen a lot of people injured with just about any kind of movement program though, I'll admit. But Yin yoga seems like a recipe for injury. I've been in Yin classes when my body told me that it had enough of the position and, as I started to come out of that position, the teacher *really* encouraged me to stay. To just "breathe and let go" and wait for the intensity to shift. But it was getting more intense!

When I was suffering with sciatica and trying desperately to stretch my piriformis, my yoga teacher would come push on my back to get me deeper into the stretch, telling me to keep relaxing more and more. Afterward I struggled to get up off the floor and, after one particularly "deep stretch," I had trouble walking for a few weeks. Relaxing and going deeper didn't work. I don't really like anyone overriding me listening to my body, frankly. So why did my body resist?

There is a protective mechanism in your muscles called the **stretch reflex** which signals the muscle to contract if a passive stretch is too long (or too fast). And that's what Yin yoga is. A passive stretch, which is a stretch you hold, trying to relax more and more into it. For a very long time.

I feel that if the stretch reflex has engaged and you feel you are getting tighter and your body yells "get outta there!" then you should listen to it. Your body protects that tissue for a reason. Maybe the muscle is weak and the fascial bag is frail and at risk of tearing. When people don't listen, they come to me for help.

They may have activated trigger points in the very muscles they were trying to release because the stretch reflex forced the muscle into contraction. I've observed that when a muscle reflexively contracts to protect itself, trigger points get more intense. Those folks ignoring their body's messages in Yin yoga (or any yoga or stretching program) end up sore and injured. I know the Yin yoga teachers are going to get mad at me for this but I have to say it! Yes, a Yin yoga practice can be an incredible tool for increasing flexibility. My concern arises when the messages from inside the body are ignored.

Out of my confusion and concern about Yin yoga, I went and studied with the source, Paulie Zink, who created many of the stretches we know as Yin yoga today. Paulie Zink is a Kung Fu master. He's amazing! And his long-held stretches were always done after rigorous training. Rigorous training engaged more parts of the muscle, got more of it contracted in a good way. Building up contraction in the muscles acts as protection around the trigger points. He told us in the training that his long-held stretches were *never intended to be done alone* without strengthening practices first. If you do a YouTube search on Paulie Zink and Yin yoga, you will find his Yin yoga practices are actually dynamic.

One of his students took the passive stretches, without the strengthening beforehand, and turned it into what is commonly known as Yin yoga today. His name is Paul Grilley. I also studied with Paul. He taught me a lot about the body, how every single person is shaped a little differently. Paul taught that everyone's bones are unique, and his training deepened my understanding of how the body works. I learned of the extraordinary variety of ways bones take shape while based on the template of the human skeleton. And yet I was always very sore, and sometimes really struggled, after Yin yoga practices.

I admit modern Yin yoga may work for some bodies, but I don't believe long-held passive stretching works for all. If your body tells you to move out of the pose, then do it. Back out a little bit. You can always go back into the stretch, perhaps just a little less. My main issue with Yin is when the teacher tells students to override the signals from inside their bodies. They cannot know how frail your fascial bags may be or how many latent trigger points are in there, ready to activate. There are excellent teachers offering Yin who *do* encourage you to listen to your body. Study with those ones.

To protect your muscle in a passive stretch you must move slowly into it, stop at the first sensation of stretch, and see how you feel. Can you breathe deeply and relax? If yes, then it's okay to stay. The key is to *listen to your body.* If your body tells you the stretch is fine, then stay and enjoy it. If your body tells you the stretch is too much and you've gone too far, you have two choices: back out a little bit or engage the muscle a little bit. Here's how that works. Sit on the floor and stretch your legs out in front of you. As you bow the torso forward, staying long through your spine and not curling inward, notice when you start to feel your hamstrings stretch. Now engage those muscles a little bit by pressing your heels into the floor.

This action lets your body know, "I'm here. I'm paying attention." You are no longer in a passive stretch triggering that protective reflex. What you'll find is that you can immediately go deeper into the stretch. Try it for yourself and see. And try that little bit of engagement in your Yin yoga classes or any time you are wanting to hang out in a stretch for several minutes. Or you can simply back out a little to reduce the intensity of the stretch. If you're stressed in the stretch, and worried about tearing something, that's not helpful. Once your body gets used to stretching, that stress response lessens, the body is less protective, and you can hold passive stretch positions for longer periods of time safely.

Yoga is amazing! I want you to fall in love with it. The benefits of yoga for the body and stress reduction have been studied over and again. It's time. Do some yoga. Check the book website for some simple yoga routines and examples of engaged stretches that you can follow. You won't believe how good you can feel at any age! And if you're not into yoga, at least do some stretching every day. Your body will thank you for it by giving you greater range of motion, less pain, and a greater sense of wellbeing.

CHAPTER 27

Freedom Point #5: Therapeutic Rolling

It seems like every gym, yoga studio, and fitness center has a basket of therapy balls and foam rollers these days. Use them! These tools have the power to transform your body in extraordinary ways and I *love* therapeutic rolling with balls and foam rollers. They helped me escape sciatica for good. They help my clients and students escape pain every day. Done regularly, therapeutic rolling is a tool to discover latent trigger points to be released and avoid pain and loss of mobility in the future. If there are active trigger points in your body, you can go directly to the source of pain and release it. If you have thirsty fascia, rolling is like a tall, cool glass of water.

SELF-MYOFASCIAL RELEASE: SMFR

Foam rolling as we typically think about it is called Self-Myofascial Release, or SMFR. From a fascia perspective, SMFR flushes the fascia and hydrates the areas you are rolling. Foam rolling increases the hydration of fascia with what's known as the "sponge effect." When you roll your fascia, you press the fluids out along the line of your rolling. That fluid includes waste products and metabolites, so this practice helps you to clean out the fascia in a way. When you go back the other direction, or release, the fascia fills back up like a sponge with fresh hydration (Schleip 2017, 93).

Fascia gets more slickery when you do therapeutic rolling. Being slick and slippery is essential for healthy fascia and healthy fascia is essential to feeling less pain and having greater mobility. The substance that makes fascia slickery is called hyaluronic acid. Hyaluronic acid is a chain of sugars that super hydrates the tissues. The Harvard Health blog, in an article on hyaluronic acid, states that "it is capable of binding over one thousand times its weight in water" (Liu and Nassim 2020). Talk about hydration!

Hyaluronic acid is produced by a newly discovered cell which has been named a **fasciacyte** (Stecco et al. 2018). Discovered in 2018, a fasciacyte is similar to a fibroblast, those cells that produce collagen and elastin which give the fibers and structure to fascia. Fasciacytes produce the slickery hyaluronic acid that keeps everything moving. Fasciacytes are stimulated to produce hyaluronic acid when put under a shearing force. This is one effect of therapeutic rolling. You can pin the tissue under the ball and rock a little, twist a little, move your body while holding the ball in place. Those movements create shear in the tissues which stimulates the production of hyaluronic acid, keeping your fascia super hydrated and keeping you mobile and pain free. SMFR using balls and foam rollers has been consistently proven to increase range of motion (Yoshimura, Schleip, and Hirose 2020).

SELF-TRIGGER-POINT RELEASE: STPR

Self-Trigger-Point Release is like foam rolling on steroids. STPR gives you the power to find and release your trigger points, immediately increasing strength and mobility while also decreasing or eliminating pain. With STPR you don't just roll around and hope for the best, you go directly to the source of your issues and work them out. To be effective in that way you need a guide, which is why I started my YouTube channel, www.YouTube.com/@CatMatlock. *The Trigger Point Therapy Workbook* by Clair and Amber Davies is a self-trigger-point release manual which can also serve as a guide.

Self-Trigger-Point Release is *precise*. Trigger points develop in patterned ways so you roll where trigger points typically tend to form and see if you've got any there. The trigger point and pain referral maps are helpful. It's also helpful to understand how muscles work together and which groups to address in the same rolling session for maximum benefit. In a nutshell, think opposing muscle groups, such as release both the quadricep and the hamstring groups in the same session. These are the kinds of things you can learn from my YouTube channel.

When you practice STPR, you learn the specific places where tension is held inside your body. Everyone's body has unique patterns of tension and you need to discover yours to maintain mobility and decrease pain. When you start rolling around, you not only find the active trigger points causing you pain, but you can also locate those sneaky latent trigger points from past injuries. Then if you do slip and fall, your body won't pull that old tensional recipe card and take on the shape and pain of injuries from long ago. You don't freak out in fear. You won't panic because you'll have some skills to nurture yourself out of the injury, like I did when I hurt my back last year. Remember that story? I immediately took some deep breaths, told myself I was going to be okay, got down on the floor, and did some slow movement. I gently rolled on balls to release my fascia and trigger points. I was fine in about a week.

I ran into a former client who I hadn't seen in years. She used to have chronic and debilitating pain all the time but now she's free. After hugs and catching up on all her foster kittens and rescue dogs, she shared that when her neck gets tweaked, she knows exactly what to do. She explained that her freedom from constant pain came partly due to knowing how to release her own trigger points and partly due to not catastrophizing her pain. Yep. Downgrading the stress response, not going into fear, and dealing with your trigger points. It works. She recalled that the last time I had seen her, I ended our session by saying, "You are safe."

Pretty much everyone needs therapeutic rolling. I have helped thousands of people fix debilitating, acute, and persistent pains. Some people I've helped I've never met personally because they follow my YouTube channel and send me comments, emails, or text messages. One eighty-four-year-old man just messaged me last week. He had been locked up in pain and practically immobile for weeks until he found my channel. He followed my videos, used a tennis ball, and was back to being 99 percent fully functional and pain free. I'd never even met him. And he's eighty-four! That's the power of this work. I hear these stories all the time.

Therapeutic rolling truly has the power to transform your body out of pain. When I work with someone in person, during my lower back and sciatica coaching program, or online during private coaching, I give them a set of balls to work with and send them a protocol of videos to follow for their homework. Now, through the channel and online offerings, I get to help people all over the world, which is really cool. I love my job!

I want my clients to work on themselves at home because trigger points can be so darned persistent. Habits die hard and habits of contraction (trigger points) are no different. Trigger points come back and often need more than one treatment. My clients release their trigger points a little bit every day and after a short while, sometimes within a few days, the body gets the message and the trigger point doesn't come back. They recover much faster if they do slip or fall. I also observe that they feel empowered in understanding how their bodies work, and they don't get as afraid when they tweak something. Feeling empowered is a huge SIM, Safety In Me. The more SIMs, the less pain. Having an understanding of therapeutic rolling, SMFR and STPR, is a SIM.

WHAT TOOLS SHOULD I USE?

THERAPY BALLS AND FOAM ROLLERS

I recommend you have a little assortment of therapy balls to use on your body. You'll need balls of various sizes and firmness. You need a soft ball, like the air-filled FreeBody ball, for your belly and front of the neck. You *must* have a soft ball. You can use that soft ball everywhere on your body because it's gentle and trigger points hurt when you press on them. The soft ball is also excellent for shear and fascial health.

A soft ball is necessary in the belly and parts of the neck because you don't want to put a hard ball in those areas due to risk of damaging delicate structures. As I mentioned in the discussion on stress and back pain, please do not use a lacrosse ball under a kettlebell in your psoas, the largest hip flexor which lies deep in the belly along the lumbar spine. I cringe when I see that. There are nerves and blood supply and organs in there! I recommend staying away from a lacrosse ball altogether. A lacrosse ball is basically a stone, and if you use that, you blast past a bunch of soft-touch sensory receptors, the ones that soothing massage communicates with and which foster good feelings of wellbeing.

If you use too hard of a ball, or too firm of a foam roller, you might be causing your body to protect itself with more contraction, undermining your efforts. Amber Davies said she gives her clients a choice of balls to take with them and, after trying a variety, only a few take her up on the lacrosse ball. I'm thin, and a lacrosse ball is simply too hard to use anywhere on my body. I appreciate that bigger-bodied folks will need a firmer ball than I need in thicker areas, like the hips. Yet, a lacrosse ball is too firm for most people. It's definitely too hard for your belly and neck! I made a video about that which you can watch on the website to learn more about it.

Think about this for a minute. When you are going to receive a massage because you are feeling pain somewhere, do you want your massage therapist to walk in and start digging their elbows as hard as they can into your most tender places without any warming up or soothing first? No. You eventually want them to get to those tender places, yes, but your body isn't ready for such deep work at the start, especially if it's protecting an injury. I've had this experience and made the therapist stop because they were hurting me. It's not helpful. The same is true with self-massage using balls and tools. You don't want to just hammer away at a spot that's inflamed and hurt. Your body will respond with protecting that area by contracting tissues and perhaps with more inflammation. You've got to soothe the fascia first, hydrate the area, then slowly sink into the deeper layers. Dehydrated tissue cannot change or heal.

When doing therapeutic rolling, it is best to start gently, breathe deeply, and pay attention to how things feel. Err on the side of too little pressure, especially at first. When you find a very tender spot, take a few long, slow, deep breaths (remember that helps the entire nervous system to soften and reduces pain) and see how much you can relax, because ultimately relaxing is what you're going for. If you're clenching and trying to bear it, well... You're working against yourself. You cannot force your way into the body. You cannot force trigger points out of your body. You cannot force your body to heal and let go. That's like yelling at a child to stop crying.

GENERAL GUIDELINES FOR SMFR AND STPR

1. Start gently with a soft ball to explore.
2. Breathe slowly and deeply.
3. Avoid skin eruptions, blisters, open wounds, recent surgeries, rashes, etc.
4. Avoid putting your full weight onto a ball after a replacement surgery, such as a hip replacement, choosing to roll your hip with the ball against a wall instead.
5. Avoid areas that are red, swollen, and inflamed.
6. Avoid pressure directly on bones and joints except with a soft, air-filled ball like the FreeBody ball.
7. Go slowly, rolling up and down in long strokes to get the fascia hydrated.
8. When you find a really tender spot which may be a trigger point, sink into it, play with movement of the muscle/tissues you have pinned under the ball.
9. If you're cursing in your head or holding your breath, that's too much pressure and you need to back off.
10. Err on the side of too little pressure; be kind to your body.
11. Spend some time on your whole body, not just where it hurts, to cover whole fascial lines.
12. If you've got pain or tension somewhere, try releasing the opposite muscle groups first, or the muscles which might be pulling on the ones that have issues. For instance, when you have hip flexor tension, try first releasing the hip extensors, the hamstrings and gluteus maximus. If

you have shoulder issues, roll out the Big Three before working on any of the shoulder muscles directly.

13. Subscribe to and follow videos on my YouTube channel, @CatMatlock, so you don't have to guess where to work. Check out the playlists.

14. Be curious, have fun, enjoy getting to know your body, be grateful to your body.

15. *Gently* stretch and do some easy movement afterward.

PERCUSSION MASSAGER A.K.A. MASSAGE GUN

Percussion massagers have gotten very popular recently. When used correctly, they can offer increased range of motion and decreased pain and make it easier for you to release tension in your body (Konrad 2020). When I spoke with Stew Wild, one of my trigger point instructors who you met back in the *Trigger Point* section, he shared that he finds the percussion massager to be quite a valuable tool. I use my percussion massager in sessions with clients and often recommend they purchase one to use at home. However, I find a lot of people don't know how to use the massager well, partly because they don't know where their trigger points are and partly because our culture loves to say, "go big or go home." Folks can injure themselves using a percussion massager too aggressively. I counsel my clients to use the flat head of the massage tool instead of the "bullet" shaped one. This makes the massager less invasive. You really don't want to beat on your soft tissues with a pokey hard plastic object attached to a mechanical jackhammer. Ouch!

As percussion massagers are somewhat new on the scene, there are not a ton of studies that have been done to properly prove the effects of this tool. To make things more interesting, studies that have been done on "vibration" therapy have been carried over to prove the efficacy of "percussion" therapy and they are actually two different things. Percussion is more like that little jackhammer than a vibration tool.

With a little guidance, you can use a percussion massager at home and may perhaps find some great benefit. My clients love it and find it very useful. I counsel them to keep it charged by the couch. Whenever you sit on the couch to watch something on TV, just grab your percussion massager and work on yourself. Use it on your calves (gently here!) hamstrings, quadriceps, glutes, soles of the feet, wherever it feels good. Just be mindful and follow the guidelines below. I am currently working on a series of videos teaching people how to safely use a percussion massager. Check the book website for videos with techniques and guidance. I'll give you some of those guidelines here, the things I tell my clients when they are taking their percussion massager home for self-care.

GENERAL GUIDELINES FOR USING A PERCUSSION MASSAGER

- Use the flat or ball head instead of the bullet attachment.
- Avoid pushing the massager into your body. Keep it superficial.
- Use long strokes up and down the length of the muscle.
- When you find a tender spot, spend a little time there (without pushing) then go back to long strokes.
- Work opposing muscle groups in one session; hamstrings and quads, inner thighs and outer hips, etc.

- Avoid bones, joints, and the other stuff to avoid from above, like open wounds and recent surgeries.
- Breathe deeply and slowly.
- Do a little movement and stretching afterward.

Now that we've discussed therapeutic rolling, you've learned about all the parts of the FreeBody System and why we do what we do. The FreeBody System includes:

1. Self-regulation and practices to soothe the nervous system
2. Posture awareness and getting into Active Posture
3. Movement breaks throughout the day
4. Stretching full lines of fascia and engaged stretching
5. Therapeutic Rolling: Self-Trigger-Point Release and Self-Myofascial Release

If you attend to all five of these parts, you just may be amazed at how good you can feel at *any* age! So now you might be wondering, how do I implement this system into my day? Isn't this going to take a lot of time and practice? Not really. It may seem like a lot at first because it's a new way to look at things. Beginning something new always feels awkward and time consuming. Once you start paying attention to your posture, your breath, and stress, those become effortless and take no time at all. The movement breaks are a couple of minutes long so that's easy. Stretching and therapeutic rolling feels so good you will *want* to do them regularly. Let's see what a FreeBody day looks like as we head into our conclusion.

CHAPTER 28

A FreeBody Day

———

Here is one example of how to structure a FreeBody Day which attends to all Five Points of the FreeBody System. This template is meant to get you started in your healing process. Healing takes some time. If you're in pain right now, this template will start you on the road to settling your nervous system, unwinding you from pain, and get you moving. If you're not in pain, this practice will support you staying that way. It may look like a lot but the breaks are only about three minutes long. The entire program takes about an hour, broken up into parts throughout the day. Isn't freedom worth an hour? Add a little bit to your routine at a time. Start with the breathing and movement breaks.

As always, you should check with your health care provider and get approval before taking on any exercise program, especially if you have a herniated disc, a spondylolisthesis (one vertebra has slid forward), are pregnant (don't roll on the belly) or suffer from a systemic disease. If you're not sure, just check with your healthcare provider. Got approval? Then let's go. See the book website for videos to follow.

THE FIVE POINTS OF FREEDOM IN THE FREEBODY SYSTEM:

1. Soothe: Self-regulation and breathing practices to soothe the nervous system
2. Posture: Active Posture
3. Move: Movement breaks throughout the day
4. Stretch: Stretching full lines of fascia and engaged stretching
5. Roll: Therapeutic Rolling with Self-Trigger-Point Release and Self-Myofascial Release

A SAMPLE FREEBODY DAY

This practice is not intended for someone with a spondylolisthesis as it includes back strengthening and gentle back bending which are contraindicated for that condition. If you have a spondylolisthesis, focus on the breathing parts, move gently, and skip the back-bending movements.

This is one example of many ways to put all the pieces together.

In the morning in bed:

- Lie on your back with your knees supported by a pillow and start with some long, slow deep breaths. Picture yourself having a good day and remember something that was delightful, that brought you joy.
- Bend your knees with your feet flat on the bed, set wide apart, and slowly rock your knees side to side like "windshield wipers," noticing where things feel tight. Go up to the edge of pain, but don't push into it. Then go to the

other side. Keep breathing deep breaths and keep moving. Do this five to ten times.

- Roll onto your belly and lie flat on your belly, breathing deeply into your back. Place a pillow underneath your belly if it's not comfortable to lie flat. Breathe deeply into the back, expanding your back fascia and muscles with your inhales and softening them with your exhales.
- Come to all fours in bed and explore some slow movements: tilt and tuck your pelvis, wag your tail, play, and do what feels good to you.

Morning breathing and meditation:

Sit in the same spot every morning if possible just for five minutes. Sit up tall, reaching the crown of your head to the sky. Consider using the Insight Timer.

Take some deep belly breaths, then focus the breath into your back, expanding the back as you breathe.

Picture yourself moving freely and easily without pain. Remind your body it knows how to do that and set that program into your brain. Remember how good that feels. Be grateful for your body and send it loving kindness. Remember that your body is designed to heal and healing is what it does. Write out a story in your Joy Journal.

Morning movement:

Spend ten minutes (at least) moving. Here are some suggestions: put on your favorite music and dance, go for a walk around the block, do a ten-minute yoga routine, go to the gym, or swim. Pick something you like to do so you'll keep doing it. Reprogram the idea of "exercise" into "movement." Just move.

Throughout your day:

At the top of every hour check your *posture*. Are you in Active Posture or are you slouching with your butt tucked underneath you? Sit up tall and don't slouch on the couch or in your chair.

Movement breaks:

Use the Pomodoro, or similar app, to schedule breaks every thirty to forty-five minutes. Here are some ideas for movement breaks. There are a bunch more on the website and YouTube channel and please feel free to make up your own. Ask your body how it wants you to move. Listen to the answer.

Break One: Take two long, slow, deep belly breaths.

Standing leg swings: Stand at the side of your chair, hand on the chair for support, and swing one leg front to back for a minute, then do the other side.

Shoulder openers: Pretend you're doing the backstroke, open your arms wide, and look up to the sky while squeezing your shoulder blades together. Shake your arms out.

Break Two: Take two long, slow, deep belly breaths.

Engaged hamstring stretch: Place a chair next to a counter or wall, stand off to the side, and place one heel on the seat of the chair and place hands on the counter or wall for support. Flex the foot on the chair and press the heel into the seat just a little bit. Bow forward to stretch the back of the leg and thigh. Keep a little pressure of the heel into the seat.

Neck ROM: Now stand tall and do some neck range of motion ten times each: nod up and down, shake your head no, tilt side to side, and slide your head forward and back.

Break Three: Take two long, slow, deep belly breaths.

Wide angle side to side: Stand in front of your chair, place your hands on the chair seat and step your feet wide. Now bend the right knee, keeping the left knee straight, then bend the left knee and straighten the right one. Go back and forth for a minute or two.

Funky hip dance: Now stand tall, step your feet a little wide, hands to your hips, lift one hip and then the other like you're wagging your tail side to side. Do for about a minute. Bonus points for blasting funky music at the same time.

Break Four: Take two long, slow, deep belly breaths.

Locust pose: This break is more advanced so only do it if it doesn't cause pain. Lie on the floor on your belly. As you inhale, lift your upper body off the floor to strengthen the back. Lift and lower five times, lifting on the inhale and lowering on the exhale.

Dance party: Just dance!

Break Five: Take two long, slow, deep belly breaths.

Squats: Stand up and do some easy squats (or do them every time you brush your teeth)

Chair lift or hand weights: Stand behind your chair and lift it up over your head, take a few breaths, then put it down. If that seems like a terrible idea, keep a set of three-, five-, or eight-pound weights nearby. Hold one in each hand and lift over your head, then take a few deep breaths.

Repeat throughout the day. Mix and match. Make up your own practices. Enjoy.

Self-Myofascial Release/Self-Trigger-Point Release:

Psoas release: When you get home, lie face down on the floor with the soft FreeBody ball under the right side of your belly, about an inch away from your navel. Take some deep breaths. Rock your body a little side to side as you breathe and sink for three to five breaths. Then do the same on the left side.

Full fascial line stretch: Cobra pose: Begin on the floor on your belly. Place your elbows or hands on the floor in front of you and lift your upper body off the floor so you are propped up on your belly and elbows/hands. Avoid pushing up if painful. Stay here for five breaths. Alternatively, you can do a standing back bend where you just lift your arms up and arch your back a little, strengthening the back and opening the belly.

TLF and Lumbar Release: Get up and grab a small ball, about the size of a tennis ball, or the soft FreeBody ball available on the book website. Step with your back to a wall, ball in your hand. Stand with your back and buttocks against the wall, feet stepped a little forward. The further you step your feet away, the more pressure in the ball. The closer you stand to the wall, the less pressure. Adjust accordingly and remember, start with just a little pressure and work your way to deeper pressure, so stand closely at first.

Place that ball next to, but not on, the lumbar spine. Roll along the spine, rolling the ball up and down by bending and straightening your knees as the ball moves up and down along the muscles and fascia. Picture the thoracolumbar fascia and imagine rolling on it. Get a nice smooth rhythm, slowly rolling up and down along the sides of the lumbar spine. After about a minute on one side, focus on very tender spots. Sink in, take some deep breaths. Repeat on the other side. Be gentle! Step closer to the wall. Remember, if it hurts a lot, your body will respond with more protection: trigger points, inflammation, and stress.

Cat/cow movement Come to all fours with your hands shoulder distance apart and your knees hip distance apart.

Inhale, drop your belly, stick your butt up and back behind you, and look forward. Exhale, gently round your back a little bit, slightly tucking your pelvis under. Avoid overdoing this part if you have back pain! Focus on the inhale portion. For the exhale portion, you can return back to neutral position.

Still on all fours, wag your tail side to side.

Consider purchasing a **percussion massager** and keep it beside your couch. Whenever you watch a show, use it gently on your hamstrings, glutes, quads on the front of the thigh, inner thighs, feet, calves, etc.

Evening practice before bed:

Sit in the same spot every evening if possible. Sit up tall, reaching the crown of your head to the sky.

Take some deep belly breaths then focus the breath into your back, expanding the back as you breathe.

Follow a twenty- to thirty-minute guided meditation program such as are available on the Insight Timer or from the book website.

At the end of the guided practice, picture yourself moving freely and easily without pain. Remind your body it knows how to do that and set that program into your brain. Remember how good that feels. Be grateful for your body and send it loving kindness.

Conclusion: Hope

You don't have to do it alone, but you do have to do it yourself.

Self-care is truly not optional. And you have to do it yourself. No one is inside your body and your experiences but you. I wish to empower you to listen to your body in a new way. When we ignore our bodies we lose mobility, we feel pain, we suffer. But suffering doesn't have to be your story. The human body is a miraculous healing wonder! Given the opportunity, healing is what it does. Pain in our bodies is a signal of protection. Pain says, "Something is off either physically or emotionally or both. Please pay attention." That's really what pain and dysfunction are asking of us, our attention and care. Now that you understand a little bit about trigger points and muscles, a little bit about fascia, and a little bit about stress and the brain, and how those things relate to each other, then you can bring your informed attention to the conversation. You can listen with a greater ability to respond well to your body's messages.

Through our bodies we feel and process our entire emotional landscape. Our difficult emotions feel like physical pain. We feel heartache as real physical pain. Grief can feel like a crushing weight on the chest. New love can feel like an energizing, radiating ecstasy, and it dissolves pain. When there have been difficult, scary, or traumatic experiences, sometimes we get stuck in protection mode and we feel that fear, worry, or sadness regularly. Or we just feel pain. When we worry about an injury that keeps coming back, that worry is always with us, gripping our muscles and fascia, creating trigger points and weakness, and that old injury returns again. Physical pain creates emotional stress. Emotional stress creates physical pain. It becomes challenging to see the way out, and so we get stuck.

But we don't have to get stuck. Freedom is real, possible, and available to you right now. I'm here to ring the bell of hope! I have healed trauma and its corresponding lower back pain in my own body. I healed chronic debilitating sciatica. I'm free! And you can do it, too. I have witnessed literally thousands of people heal just about everything, from a chronically weak ankle years after an original sprain to seventy years of persistent headaches to deep terrifying trauma that led to the whole body seizing up in pain. The FreeBody Method serves everyone, no matter your age or condition. Every body can feel better with attention and care.

If you want more support, I encourage you to subscribe to my YouTube channel as I'm constantly putting out new videos, adding to the hundreds that are already there. Find me on YouTube @CatMatlock.

If you are a massage therapist and wish to have clarity on treating trigger points and pain from a trauma informed approach, subscribe to my YouTube channel devoted to body-work practitioners @FreeBodyMassage.

Go to the website www.FreeBodyBook.com and you'll find a bunch of resources and videos to support what you've learned.

Schedule a Telehealth session and meet with me online to receive a curated protocol of videos to follow based on your symptoms and needs. Link is available on the book website.

Got lower back or sciatica pain? That's my specialty. Please join my Low Back Liberation coaching program. I will show you the exact steps people in chronic low back or sciatica pain need to take to be pain free, or at least 85 percent better, in about ninety days without surgery, drugs, endless appointments, or confusion.

Take a retreat with me to sink in, learn how to release your trigger points, practice proven techniques to tame your Inner Neanderthal, stretch, and deeply listen to what your body is telling you. Again, you do have to do it yourself, but you don't have to do it alone. I want to show you how.

If you work in a corporate environment, hire me to come and help your team learn skills to decompress, get out of a stress response, and get back into flow. When teams use the FreeBody System, creativity and productivity improve dramatically and folks miss far less work due to pain and illness. Everybody wins.

I truly look forward to meeting you, working with you, and helping you to get back to living the good life you are meant to live.

Now, take a long, slow, deep breath. Relax your muscles. Feel the seat you are on, holding you up, supporting you. Place a hand over your heart or somewhere on your body. Offer some kindness to yourself and your body. Picture yourself moving freely and easily. Allow hope inside.

Welcome to FreeBody.

Acknowledgments

Special thanks to my daughter, Kayla Matlock Schmitt, for your encouragement. My dear Kayla, I love you to the moon and back. I am proud of you every single day.

I send deep gratitude to my parents, Bob and Dana Matlock, for all your support and love.

Shout out to my brothers, Rick and Tim Matlock, my nephew, James Matlock, and my cousin, Kelly Smith.

Thank you family!

Thank you to Gil Hedley, Stew Wild, Amber Davies, Kristine Kaoverii Weber and Althea Wilkins for taking time to let me interview you. Thank you to Eddy Sampson for creating the pain referral images for this book. This book would be incomplete without your expertise.

Big shout out to the team at Manuscripts Modern Author Accelerator and www.Manuscripts.com. Thank you to all the instructors, guides, and editors I worked with along the way. Wow. We did it! I appreciate you all!

Big thanks to those who believed in me enough to pre-purchase this book. Thank you! I truly hope it serves you.

Nemesia Sorcar, Andrew Bednarzik, Tēfa Hallock, Erin Brittain, Jillian Isele, Nira Stulck, Becks Logan, Lisa Sherman, Alice Eacho, Caryn Hanna, Vicky Bricker, Jill Gottesman, Deborah Mills, Andrea Debevoise, Julie Matthews, Samata Decori, Raphaela Fritz, Sandy Newes, Michael Newes, Maria Mendola Shamas, Mary Morgan, Shannon South, Marisa Blake, Eric Koester, April Delac, Shar'ron Boren, Alexis Rosenfelt, Mado Hesselink, Carla White, Robin Funsten, Jeni Bittner-Hughey, Libby Hinsley, Maurice Legendre, Austyn Mcallister, Zachary Kilberg, Matt Howell, Tracey Schmidt, Danielle Cain, Nick D'souza, Jae Friedman, Christie Melear, Stan Mogelnicki, Terri Reed, Carole Vacher, Carolyn Baker, Shannon Carney, Ryan Pickens, Holly Hight, Dianne Lancaster, Cindy Levine, Sheryne Glicksman, Jillian Balderson, Michael Swanson, Janis Williams, Robin Fann, Sara Kull, Dennis Kozak, Brandi Hubiak, Quinn Scobie, Cynthia Waggoner, Sierra Hollister, Denise Fortier, Ann Rogers, John Phillips, Erica Carroll, Marianne Fox, Audrey Long, Valerie Kula, Valerie Stone, Kirk Neumann, Amy Howard, Michelle Francis, Beth Bluth, Dorothy Booraem, Shealy Thompson, Lindsay Heller, Sarah Tambor, Deborah Menagh, Luna Canter, Mike Vance, Lauren Duhe, Jill Jones, Karen Hardison, Eileen Gertz, Lizzy Ziogas, Lee Warren, Taija Ventrella, Zoe Schumaker, Brian Relph, Rosie Mulford, Stephanie Metzger, Huma Mcauley, Linnea Linton, Marin Leroy, April Leasure, Josh Kelly, Stephanie Howarth, Deana

Johnson, Cathy Eising, Nat Cohen, Wes Burke, Brotherhug Barlow, Michelle Assoian, Alice Arthur, Nicole "Pickles" Mcclane, Stacy Claude, Brian Loftin, Kate Shelton, Wendy Begonis, Cameron Richardson, Lillah Schwartz, Christina Madden, Connie Scrivens, Kristina Berkeley, Mikaila Mills, and Melina Ulrich.

Appendix

———

INTRODUCTION

Dieleman, Joseph, Jackie Cao, Abby Chapin, Carina Chen, Zhi-yin Li, Angela Liu, Cody Horst, Alexander Kaldjian, Taylor Matyasz, and Kirstin Woody Scott, et al. 2020. "US Health Care Spending by Payer and Health Condition, 1996–2016." *Journal of the American Medical Association,* 323, (March): 863-884. DOI 10.1001/jama.2020.0734.

US Department of Health and Human Services. 2020. "Opioid Facts and Statistics." US Dept. of Health and Human Services. Accessed November 17, 2022. https://www.hhs.gov/opioids/statistics/index.html.

CHAPTER 2: WHAT IS A TRIGGER POINT?

Davies, Clair, and Amber Davies. 2004. *The Trigger Point Therapy Workbook: Your Self-Treatment Guide for Pain Relief.* Oakland: New Harbinger Press.

Debold, E. P., S. E. Beck, and D. M. Warshaw. 2008. "Effect of Low pH on Single Skeletal Muscle Myosin Mechanics and Kinetics." *American Journal of Physiology: Cell Physiology* 295, no. 1 (July): C173–9. DOI: 10.1152/ajpcell.00172.2008.

Hultman, E., and P. L. Greenhaff. 1991. "Skeletal Muscle Energy Metabolism and Fatigue during Intense Exercise in Man." *Science Progress* 75, 298: 361–70.

Journal of Clinical Orthodontics. 1989. "Janet G. Travell, MD on Myofascial Pain" *JCO* Interviews. Accessed June 30, 2023. https://www.jco-online.com/archive/1989/07/468-jco-interviews-janet-g-travell-md-on-myofascial-pain/.

Lin, Jiann-Her ,Chih-Hsien Hung, Der-Sheng Han, Shih-Ting Chen, Cheng-Han Lee, Wei-Zen Sun, and Chih-Cheng Chen. 2018. "Sensing Acidosis: Nociception or Sngception?" *Journal of Biomedical Science* 25, no. 85 (November). https://doi.org/10.1186/s12929-018-0486-5.

Shah, Jay P., Jerome V. Danoff, Mehul J. Desai, Sagar Parikh, Lynn Y. Nakamura, Terry M. Phillips, and Lynn H. Gerber. 2008.

"Biochemicals Associated with Pain and Inflammation Are Elevated in Sites Near to and Remote from Active Myofascial Trigger Points." *Archives of Physical Medicine and Rehabilitation,* 89, (January): 16–23. DOI 10.1016/j.apmr.2007.10.018.

Travell, Janet G., David G. Simons, and Lois S. Simons. 1999. *Travell and Simons' Myofascial Pain and Dysfunction: The Trigger Point Manual. Vol. 1 - Upper Half of Body.* 2nd Edition. Baltimore: Lippincott Williams & Wilkins.

CHAPTER 3: TYPES OF TRIGGER POINTS

Mense, Siegfried, and David G. Simons. 2001. *Muscle Pain: Understanding Its Nature, Diagnosis, and Treatment*. Baltimore: Lippincott Williams & Wilkins.

Travell, Janet G., David G. Simons, and Lois S. Simons. 1999. *Travell and Simons' Myofascial Pain and Dysfunction: The Trigger Point Manual. Vol. 1 - Upper Half of Body*. 2nd Edition. Baltimore: Lippincott Williams & Wilkins.

CHAPTER 4: TRIGGER POINT SYMPTOMS

Travell, Janet G., David G. Simons, and Lois S. Simons. 1999. *Travell and Simons' Myofascial Pain and Dysfunction: The Trigger Point Manual. Vol. 1 - Upper Half of Body*. 2nd Edition. Baltimore: Lippincott Williams & Wilkins.

CHAPTER 5: SCIATICA AND TRIGGER POINTS

Travell, Janet G., and David G. Simons. 1993. *Myofascial Pain and Dysfunction: The Trigger Point Manual. Vol. 2 - The Lower Extremities*. Philadelphia: Lippincott Williams & Wilkins.

CHAPTER 8: WHAT IS FASCIA

Brooks, George A., and Glenn A. Gaesser. 1980. "End Points of Lactate and Glucose Metabolism after Exhausting Exercise." *Journal of Applied Physiology*, 49, (December): 1057-1069. DOI: 10.1152/jappl.1980.49.6.1057.

Myers, Thomas. 2001. *Anatomy Trains*. London: Churchill Livingstone.

Wilke, Jan, and Michael Behringer. 2021. "Is 'Delayed Onset Muscle Soreness' a False Friend? The Potential Implication of the Fascial Connective Tissue in Post-Exercise Discomfort." *International Journal of Molecular Sciences*, 22, (August). DOI: 10.3390/ijms22179482.

CHAPTER 9: FASCIA AND LOWER BACK PAIN

Dommerholt, Jan. 2012. "Trigger Point Therapy" In *Fascia*, edited by Robert Schleip, Thomas W. Findley, Leon Chaitow, Peter A. Huijing. 297–302. London: Churchill Livingstone.

Hoheisel, U., J. Rosner, and S. Mense. "Innervation Changes Induced by Inflammation of the Rat Thoracolumbar Fascia." 2015. *Neuroscience*, 300, (August): 351–359. DOI: 10.1016/j.neuroscience.2015.05.034.

Jensen, M. C., M. N. Brant-Zawadzki, N. Obuchowski, M. T. Modic, D. Malkasian, and J. S. Ross. 1994. "Magnetic Resonance Imaging of the Lumbar Spine in People without Back Pain." *New England Journal of Medicine,* 331, (July): 69–73. DOI: 10.1056/ NEJM199407143310201.

Lowe, Whitney, and Til Luchau. 2021. "Fascia in Sport and Movement." *The Thinking Practitioner Podcast*. Released September 28, 2021. 1hr 10 mins. https://www.academyofclinicalmassage. com/podcast/.

Meert, Guido F. 2012. "Fluid Dynamics in Fascial Tissues." In *Fascia*, edited by Robert Schleip, Thomas W. Findley, Leon Chaitow, Peter A. Huijing, 177–181. London: Churchill Livingstone.

Schleip, Robert. 2017. *Fascial Fitness*. West Sussex: Lotus Publishing.

Travell, Janet, David G. Simons, and Lois Simons. 1999. Travell and Simons' Myofascial Pain and Dysfunction: The Trigger Point Manual. Vol. 1 - Upper Half of Body. 2nd Edition. Baltimore: Lippincott Williams & Wilkins.

Vleeming, Andry. 2012. "The Thoracolumbar Fascia" In *Fascia*, edited by Robert Schleip, Thomas W. Findley, Leon Chaitow, Peter A. Huijing, 37–43. London: Churchill Livingstone.

World Health Organization. 2022. "Musculoskeletal Health." July 14, 2022. https://www.who.int/news-room/fact-sheets/detail/musculoskeletal-conditions.

CHAPTER 10: THE MAGICAL MORPHING JELL-O INSIDE YOU

Krystel-Whittemore, Melissa, Kottarappat N. Dileepan, and John G. Wood. 2016. "Mast Cell: A Multi-Functional Master Cell." *Frontiers in Immunology*, 6. DOI: 10.3389/fimmu.2015.00620.

Schleip, Robert. 2017. *Fascial Fitness*. West Sussex: Lotus Publishing.

Van den Berg, Frans. 2012. "The Physiology of Fascia." In *Fascia*, edited by Robert Schleip, Thomas W. Findley, Leon Chaitow, Peter A. Huijing, 149–155. London: Churchill Livingstone.

CHAPTER 12: STRESS, TRAUMA, AND PAIN

Berkowitz, Steven J. 2023. "What Makes an Event Traumatic for a Child?" (Updated February 3, 2023) Child Mind Institute. Accessed May 27, 2023. https://childmind.org/article/makes-event-traumatic-child/.

Chu, Brianna, Komal Marwaha, Terrence Sanvictores, and Derek Ayers. 2001. "Physiology: Stress Reaction" StatPearls Internet. Accessed September 12, 2022. https://www.ncbi.nlm.nih.gov/books/NBK541120/.

CHAPTER 13: THE STRESS RESPONSE

Maydych, Viktoriya. 2019. "The Interplay between Stress, Inflammation, and Emotional Attention: Relevance for Depression." *Frontiers in Neuroscience*, 13, 384 (April 24). DOI: 10.3389/fnins.2019.00384.

Porges, Stephen W. 2009. "The Polyvagal Theory: New Insights into Adaptive Reactions of the Autonomic Nervous System." *Cleveland Clinic Journal of Medicine* 76, (April): Supplement 2, 86-90. DOI: 10.3949/ccjm.76.s2.17.

Scott, Elizabeth. 2020. "How Your Body Uses Epinephrine in Stress Response." VeryWell Mind. Accessed December 18, 2022. https://www.verywellmind.com/what-is-epinephrine-3145108#.

CHAPTER 14: THE AMYGDALA AND DANGER IN ME

Moseley, Lorimer. 2018. "Pain, the Brain, and Your Amazing Protectometer – Lorimer Moseley." Musculoskeletal Australia. December 4, 2018. 1hr 23min. https://youtu.be/lCF1_FsoonM.

Travell, Janet, David G. Simons, and Lois Simons. 1999. Travell and Simons' Myofascial Pain and Dysfunction: The Trigger Point Manual. Vol. 1 - Upper Half of Body. 2nd Edition. Baltimore: Lippincott Williams & Wilkins.

CHAPTER 15: STRESS AND YOUR BACK AND NECK

Joseph, A. E., R. N. Moman, R. A. Barman, D. J. Kleppel, N. D. Eberhart, D. J. Gerberi, M. H. Murad, and W. M. Hooten. 2022. "Effects of Slow Deep Breathing on Acute Clinical Pain in Adults: A Systematic Review and Meta-Analysis of Randomized Controlled Trials." *Journal of Evidence-Based Integrative Medicine,* 27, (Jan–Dec). DOI:10.1177/2515690X221078006.

Travell, Janet, and David Simons. 1993. *Myofascial Pain and Dysfunction: The Trigger Point Manual. Vol. 2 - The Lower Extremities.* Philadelphia: Lippincott Williams & Wilkins.

Travell, Janet, David G. Simons, and Lois Simons. 1999. *Travell and Simons' Myofascial Pain and Dysfunction: The Trigger Point Manual. Vol. 1 - Upper Half of Body.* 2nd Edition. Baltimore: Lippincott Williams & Wilkins.

CHAPTER 19: POSTURE AND NECK PAIN

Aliberti, Sara, Pietro Invernizzi, Raffaele Scurati, and Tiziana D'Isanto. 2020. "Posture and Skeletal Muscle Disorders of the Neck Due to the Use of Smartphones." *Journal of Human Sport and Exercise,* 15, (3proc), S586-S598. DOI:10.14198/jhse.2020.15.Proc3.11.

Myers, Thomas. 2001. *Anatomy Trains.* London: Churchill Livingstone.

CHAPTER 20: THE POSTURES OF SCIATICA AND HIP PAIN

Travell, Janet, and David Simons. 1993. *Myofascial Pain and Dysfunction: The Trigger Point Manual. Vol. 2 - The Lower Extremities.* Philadelphia: Lippincott Williams & Wilkins

CHAPTER 21: POSTURE, SITTING, AND BACK PAIN

Roffey, D. M., E. K. Wai, P. Bishop, B. K. Kwon, and S. Dagenais. 2010. "Causal Assessment of Occupational Sitting and Low Back Pain: Results of a Systematic Review." *Spine Journal,* 10, 3 (March): 252–261. DOI: 10.1016/j.spinee.2009.12.005.

Travell, Janet G., David G. Simons, and Lois S. Simons. 1999. *Travell and Simons' Myofascial Pain and Dysfunction: The Trigger Point Manual. Vol. 1 - Upper Half of Body.* 2nd Edition. Baltimore: Lippincott Williams & Wilkins.

CHAPTER 23: FREEDOM POINT #1; SOOTHE YOUR BRAIN

Komori T. 2018. "The Relaxation Effect of Prolonged Expiratory Breathing." *Mental Illness Journal.* 2018, 10, no. 1 (May 16): 7669. DOI: 10.4081/mi.2018.7669.

Mercadante, Anthony A., and Prasanna Tadi. 2022. "Neuroanatomy, Gray Matter." StatPearls Internet. Accessed January 15, 2023. https://www.ncbi.nlm.nih.gov/books/NBK553239/.

CHAPTER 25: FREEDOM POINT #3; MOVE

Jones, Leon C., Michelle Cleary, Rebecca Lopez, Ron Zuri, and Richard Lopez. 2008. "Active Dehydration Impairs Upper and Lower Body Anaerobic Muscular Power." *Journal of Strength and Conditioning Research,* 22, No. 2, (March): 455–463. DOI: 10.1519/JSC.ob013e3181635ba5.

Laskowski, Edward. 2022. "What Are the Risks of Sitting Too Much?" *Healthy Lifestyle-Adult Health* (Blog), Mayo Clinic Website. July 13, 2022. https://www.mayoclinic.org/healthy-lifestyle/adult-health/expert-answers/sitting/faq-2005 8005#.

Magown, Victoria. 2017. "Fascia Manipulation: Function & Treatment." MyoRehab Seminars. Accessed June 1, 2023. Webinar, 1:08:48. http://webinars.fasciamanipulation.myorehab.com/.

CHAPTER 26: FREEDOM POINT #4; STRETCHING

Myers, Thomas. 2001. *Anatomy Trains*. London: Churchill Livingstone.

CHAPTER 27: FREEDOM POINT #5; THERAPEUTIC ROLLING

Konrad A., C. Glashüttner, M. M. Reiner, D. Bernsteiner, and M. Tilp. 2020. "The Acute Effects of a Percussive Massage Treatment with a Hypervolt Device on Plantar Flexor Muscles' Range of Motion and Performance." *Journal of Sports Science Medicine* 19, no. 4 (November): 690–694. https://www.jssm.org/volume19/iss4/cap/jssm-19-690.pdf.

Liu, Kristina, and Janelle Nassim. 2020. "The Hype on Hyaluronic Acid." *Harvard Health Blog*. January 23, 2020. https://www.health.harvard.edu/blog/the-hype-on-hyaluronic-acid-2020012318653.

Schleip, Robert. 2017. *Fascial Fitness*. West Sussex: Lotus Publishing.

Stecco, Carla, Catarina Fede, Veronica Macchi, Andrea Porzionato, Lucia Petrelli, Carlo Biz, Robert Stern, and Rafaelle De Caro. 2018. "The Fasciacytes: A New Cell Devoted to Fascial Gliding

Regulation." *Clinical Anatomy* 31, (July): 667-676. DOI: 10.1002/ca.23072.

Yoshimura, Akane, Robert Schleip, and Norikazu Hirose. 2020. "Effects of Self-Massage Using a Foam Roller on Ankle Range of Motion and Gastrocnemius Fascicle Length and Muscle Hardness: A Pilot Study." *Journal of Sport Rehabilitation* 29, (February): 1171–1178. Accessed May 30, 2023. https://doi.org/10.1123/jsr.2019-0281.

www.ingramcontent.com/pod-product-compliance
Lightning Source LLC
Chambersburg PA
CBHW070852160726
48004CB00003B/1040